Old Problems in New Times

URBAN STRATEGIES FOR THE 1990s

Oliver Byrum

Sponsored by Center for Urban and Regional Affairs
University of Minnesota

Planners Press
American Planning Association
1313 E. 60th St.
Chicago, IL 60637

Second edition.
Copyright 1992 by the American Planning Association
1313 E. 60th St.
Chicago, IL 60637

ISBN (paperback edition): 0-918286-79-4
ISBN (hardbound edition): 0-918286-80-8

Library of Congress Catalog Number: 92-73811

*The first edition of this book was published by the
Center for Urban and Regional Affairs at the University
of Minnesota. Established in 1968, the center supports
university faculty and graduate students working on
research projects and technical assistance programs
growing out of major issues in the state. These issues
include local economic development, housing, education, transportation, land use, and social and human
services. In most cases, the center's projects are carried
out with individuals or groups outside the university—
often from the public sector.*

Table of Contents

Preface

In 1989 the Center For Urban and Regional Affairs at the University of Minnesota, in a project funded primarily by the McKnight Foundation, provided an opportunity to research central city planning strategies to better understand the contradictions between the well-being, potential and success of many central city improvement efforts and the continuing decline of social conditions in other parts of the cities. This report is the result of that project.

Chapter One is a summary of research carried out and of the entire report. Chapter Two discusses the market and public policy causes of inner city conditions in metropolitan areas. Chapter Three is a synopsis of the six-point metropolitan and city strategy I believe is needed to begin permanent improvement of those conditions. Chapters Four through Nine each cover one element of that six-point strategy.

In this report much is presented and asserted as conclusion. In most cases this accurately represents my degree of conviction. However, public policy is never just a matter of assertion. The reader should read this report as the academic synonym for assertion—that is, an hypothesis needing examination, testing, and discussion.

I would like to thank the City of Minneapolis for providing me a leave of absence; the University of Minnesota and the Center for Urban and Regional Affairs (CURA) for employing me during that period; Peter Hutchinson for very early seeing the potential importance of this work and encouraging it; Russ Ewald, Nancy Latimer and the McKnight Foundation for trusting in the value of this research; Thomas Scott, Thomas Anding and Shirley Bennett of CURA for logistical and substantive collaboration; Barbara Lukermann, Phil Meinenger, Judith Martin, Richard Bolan, Gary Miller, Chuck Neerland, Chuck Whiting, Marie Manthey, Sylvia Byrum, Bill Carter for reviewing evolving drafts of these ideas; and CURA staff, Chris McKee, Judith Weir and Louise Duncan, for their skilled professional editing, design, and keyboard work in preparing this book for publication. Much of the data analysis was done by Jerry Schwinghammer, of CURA. As editor, Susan Williams patiently and with great skill brought these words into a readable state.

This book is the result of thinking stimulated by reading, analysis, discussion and looking at cities. Many fellow thinkers and practitioners of city planning were essential to that process as I visited their cities. An incomplete list includes: Ernest Freeman, first as Planning Director in Cincinnati and then in Baltimore; Herb Stevens, retired Planning Director of Cincinnati; Al Barry and Larry Reich of the Baltimore Planning Department; Guy Hager of the Baltimore Regional Council of Governments; Trudy McFall of the Maryland Community Development Agency; Jane Downing, Planning Director, and Bill Farmer, Deputy Director and Chuck Carlson of the Pittsburgh Planning Department; Bob Pease and Carol Weir of the Allegheny Conference on Community Development; Bob Lurcott of the Pittsburgh Cultural Trust; Stephen Leeper of the Urban Redevelopment Authority of Pittsburgh; Stuart Reller of the Indianapolis Department of Metropolitan Development; Norm Abbott, Michael Harrison, Rodney O'Hiser and Bob Stacy of the Portland Planning Department; Ethan Selzer of the Metropolitan Planning Agency in Portland; Patrick La Crosse of the Portland Development Commission; John Carroll of Prendergast and Associates; Karl Abbott of Portland State University; Lyle Balderson of the Spokane Planning Department; Linda Morris of the Spokane Regional Commission; Bill Kelley of Eastern Washington University; Richard Yukubousky, Director of the Office for Long-Range Planning and Bonnie Snedeker of the Human Services Strategic Planning Office of the City of Seattle; Bill Lamont, former director and Susan Ellerbee of the Denver Planning Office; George Schuernstal of the Denver Metropolitan Planning Agency; Herb Smith of the University of Colorado and many others who briefly or at length helped my thought process.

The late Scott Horwitz observed this writing process with friendly and supportive interest and appropriate skepticism and I wish he were here to see that it did indeed get done.

Many at the University of Minnesota were stimulants to my thinking. Prominent among these were Dr. John Adams, whose ideas, research and writing on metropolitan housing markets and Dr. John Borchert whose ideas on everything, but particularly his passing comment on the quality of public services in low income neighborhoods, started my thought processes, for which neither may wish to be responsible, though both were very helpful.

Chapter One

Old Problems in New Times

The only genuine, long range solution for what has
happened lies in an attack—mounted at every
level—upon the conditions that breed despair and
violence. All of us know what those conditions are:
ignorance, discrimination, slums, poverty, disease,
not enough jobs. We should attack these conditions—not because we are frightened by conflict,
but because we are fired by conscience. We should
attack them because there is simply no other way to
achieve a decent and orderly society in America.

Lyndon Johnson, 1967, p. xv.

The situation most threatening to the well-being of the Twin Cities
and most other United States medium-sized metropolitan areas is
the set of economic, social and physical conditions associated with
the concentrations of poverty in older residential areas of the inner
central cities. No other problem is so damaging to people's lives
nor so pervasively connected and debilitating to all other aspects of
living in and governance of central cities.

The Minneapolis-St. Paul inner cities are suffering the same
social, economic, and physical deterioration of other urban centers.
Like most cities, we have inner city concentrations of low income
and disadvantaged people and neighborhoods, for decades increasingly separated and disconnected from the metropolitan economy
and social structure. This is our central metropolitan development
issue. The Twin Cities are subject to essentially the same social,
political, and economic forces as other cities. Our response has not
been sufficiently different to get a better result.

The forces working against inner cities are simply out of scale
with our efforts. While we have successful downtown rejuvenation,
some stabilized and rejuvenated neighborhoods, and good regional
planning and action, the overall physical and social condition of
inner portions of the central cities has declined for decades.

Neighborhoods and households weakened by these long-term
trends were targets for the recession that began the 1980s, for the

job shifts and income polarization caused by national economic restructuring, for changes in tax policy, and for reductions in funding for human service programs. The Twin Cities may have felt some of these trends less and later than other cities. But the same conditions were here and losses in other places played out here. Outstate agriculture and mining losses changed job markets. The more severely hit industrial cities of the eastern United States produced opportunity-seeking migrants who became a volatile, if numerically small, addition to the situation. All of these 1980s changes combined with long-term social and economic deficiencies to sharply increase the joblessness, homelessness, crime, drug epidemic, health and education problems we now see. That this new wave of national, metropolitan, and city problems would converge in the inner cities was not surprising. The conditions that foster and concentrate social problems had been building for decades.

In this book the term "metropolitan area" is used generally to mean the entire economic social urbanized area, i.e., Minneapolis, St. Paul and suburbs, but is not a specific or precise definition. The term "central city" means the bounded municipality, i.e., the city of Minneapolis or St. Paul or Denver. "Inner city" refers to an area within, but considerably smaller and quite different from the entire central city. "Inner city" is also used as shorthand for a set of undesirable social, economic, and physical conditions that occur within that limited portion of the central city.

The purpose of the project, and this report, is to consider the nature of inner city deterioration and suggest a strategy for long-term improvement. A successful outcome would be increased strategic discussion and adoption of policies and programs that seek to deal not only with symptoms, but with underlying causes of inner city problems.

During my twelve years as Minneapolis Director of Planning, I have seen dramatic revival of the downtown, stabilization and revitalization of many neighborhoods, a relative decline in Minneapolis property tax rates, successful retail and industrial redevelopment throughout the city, and many other tangible signs of real progress. But during the same period, repeat surveys of city homeowners showed a sharp increase in the proportion expecting to leave the city. The same surveys showed that security increasingly worried city residents, crime rates had risen, income was increasingly polarized, infant mortality rates began to worsen, and some neighborhoods were becoming unlivable.

There was a clear disconnection between the progress on some fronts and the decline of social conditions in the city. The purpose of this project was to try to understand what was happening and to formulate a strategy for response. While the Minneapolis/St. Paul metropolitan areas are given the most attention, the material is intended to apply to all medium-sized United States central cities and metropolitan areas.

As a result of this work, I believe the causes of inner city conditions are not so complex or inevitable as to defy understanding and improvement. Our current dilemma has come about through a complex and powerful mix of societal and metropolitan-scale social, economic, and public policy forces. Though complex, the causes can be understood. Though powerful, the situation is not inevitable. This situation can be greatly, though not easily, quickly or inexpensively, improved. On the other hand, the present disconnection and isolation of people and areas will generate even deeper problems unless a strategy that is comprehensive enough, accurate enough, and large enough to correct the long-term accumulation of difficulties can be put in place.

These difficult social, economic and physical conditions occur in most cities, notwithstanding wide differences in economic conditions, cultural and social patterns, political climate, form and quality of city government, and past programs intended as remedies. Both similarity of problem and the inability to solve it in a wide diversity of cities confirm that the root causes are metropolitan and societal. The situation is not caused by, nor can it be solved by, city actions alone. Its universal persistence verifies that single-focused remedies are not enough, that comprehensive strategies are needed.

The problems begin with societal-scale poverty and economic and racial differences. Those financially able to move away from those unlike themselves usually do so. Metropolitan housing markets that concentrate poverty into the poorest housing of the inner city fuel this tendency. That concentration creates further poverty. National and metropolitan housing policies and markets isolate neighborhoods from metropolitan opportunity. Public service failures and community inability to respond to difficult situations in low income areas turn them into poverty production areas. The larger society disassociates itself from the situation. The cycle deepens.

Successful neighborhoods cannot thrive under these conditions. A successful neighborhood is a place where people can survive, be safe and healthy, develop their human potential, seek and find opportunity. Such a neighborhood supports rather than hinders people in their search for successful lives.

An effective strategy for successful neighborhoods must be at least metropolitan in scale, must be long-term, must address each problem and the cumulative effects of the cycle of decline. It must work on reducing the concentration of poverty, on removing the reinforcement effect of metropolitan development policy, on reconnecting isolated areas and households to greater opportunity, on

improving services in low income areas, and on reassociating
metropolitan-scale society and leadership with the problems.

Old Problems in Other Places

One part of the research for this book was to think of the Twin
Cities as one of the medium-sized metropolitan areas in the country
and consider the extent to which all of these cities find themselves
in similar situations. Depending on definitions, there are twenty to
twenty-five mid-size metropolitan areas (2,000,000 population with
central cities of 300,000 to 700,000) in the United States: Pittsburgh, Portland, Cincinnati—places smaller than New York, Los
Angeles, Chicago and Philadelphia, and larger than Des Moines.
These cities have major league sports, but probably not more than
one team per sport.

I did not visit all of these places nor conduct rigorous systematic analysis of those I visited. However, office analysis and field
work in some of these cities persuades me that along with a lot of
differences, these places do have similar characteristics that relate
to urban planning and policy.

Time spent in Baltimore, Pittsburgh, Cincinnati, Denver,
Portland, Seattle, and Indianapolis ranged from a day to a week.
These cities, along with the Twin Cities, represent a slice across the
top half of the U.S. map with moderate southern diversions. This
set of cities is not intended to be geographically or socioeconomically representative of all medium-sized metropolitan areas, but
nicely covers the old economies, the newer, coastal regions and
mid-America, and includes very different demographic conditions.

In each case, the time was used to walk and drive in downtown, the inner city, portions of the rest of the central city and some
of the metropolitan area. Some of the looking was done with city
officials, planning directors and particularly neighborhood organ-
izers and planners. Office interviews with business people,
academics and private citizen leaders filled out the time. This was
research, but by no means exhaustive or methodically exacting
research. The value is intended to flow from the application of
extensive experience in city and metropolitan public policy and
some skill in observation and synthesis, rather than a regional
method. I was looking for ideas and strategies. I wondered whether
anyone had in place an effective, comprehensive strategy for dis-
cerning and dealing with the most difficult problems.

Visits to Atlanta, Spokane, Tel Aviv, Jerusalem, and Haifa also
influenced my thinking. Imperative side trips to smaller places rang-
ing from Murray Idaho, Walla Walla Washington, Missoula and
Wibaux Montana, and Homestead Pennsylvania helped open my
eyes to contrasting presents and likely futures.

The result: observations, impressions, some old viewpoints reinforced, and some changed viewpoints. Some well-known and obvious thoughts, but thoughts worth repeating; some convictions about what is most important and what to do with this information.

In all metropolitan areas, the central cities have the largest concentrations of oldest housing. This usually is also the cheapest housing, so the central cities house the poorest and most disadvantaged people, usually in the inner portion, near the downtown.

Long-term demographic, economic, social and development trends have been reducing the relative socioeconomic status and image of central cities within their metropolitan areas. The traditional role of the central city downtown as the economic center of the metropolitan area has been significantly, sometimes absolutely, eroded.

These long-term trends were masked in the 1970s and early 1980s by some success such as downtown rejuvenation brought about by city efforts, national tax policy, and the shift toward an office-based service economy. Housing programs and a reduced demand for market city housing also helped, but less favorable long-term inner city trends persisted.

Central cities have decided advantages. Geographic and transportation system centrality to the metropolitan marketplace, jobs and employees is an inherent and permanent advantage. Central cities have name identification and are the metropolitan centers of higher education, medicine, cultural and social institutions. A large population continues to prefer living, working or shopping in the urban environment of the central city. The wealth of the country is not found in rural areas; it is concentrated in the metropolitan areas of which these cities are the center. That wealth is seemingly available to cities' economies and public needs.

The office building boom of the late 1970s and 1980s built upon the urban renewal of the 1950s and 1960s. This boom brought about the reconstruction of most downtowns as the largest and most important, but no longer dominant, commercial center in metropolitan areas.

The retail success of downtowns is more spotty. City after city is engaged in public assistance to maintain or reestablish downtown retail centers. But the reality of where the metropolitan housing market is locating potential customers and new suburban malls threatens this. Some downtown retail centers, such as Baltimore's Harbor Place, are successful and are stimulating further redevelopment. This seems to be the case when the projects and setting are unique and interesting, when parking and transit are adequate, and when the metropolitan market is strong enough and accessible to the project.

The constructing of new or expanded convention centers as the loss leader component of a strategy to strengthen central city retail and hospitality business is universal. The last business on the main street of Murray Idaho has used the same strategy, creating a bottle museum to lure tourists into its bar and grill. In Terry Montana it is the Charles Russell paintings over the bar pulling drivers off Interstate 90.

The most fundamental change in downtowns is not so much what is being constructed, but who owns downtown, its structures and businesses. In the 1970s city leaders worried about replacing family and local management with professional management, with a smaller leadership role and stake in the community. Later the concern became the transfer of real estate to foreign corporations. Now something more fundamental is taking place in those cities that have so far benefited by concentrations of corporate headquarters. The merger and acquisition mania that is substituting for real economic growth is changing these cities from headquarters centers to subsidiary centers.

This loss of the headquarters function to mega corporations with little loyalty to place does not bode well for medium-sized cities. While growth may continue, the future will be marked by sporadic and unpredictable economic blows as decisions to reorganize and relocate subsidiary functions are made at headquarters in New York, Los Angeles, London and Tokyo. It seems unlikely that this trend will be positive for Minnesota and the Twin Cities in the long run. Our salutes to the "new global economy" should perhaps be accompanied by both restraint and preparation.

The contrasts are also present among cities. There is some geographic pattern in this. In cities of middle America, economies are weaker and stimulating economic development clearly takes public policy priority over regulating development. However, in the booming coastal cities, such as San Francisco, Seattle and Washington, D.C., finding ways to manage, regulate, slow or stop development is the dominant public issue. Portland is an anomaly, a coastal city of slow growth with much emphasis upon development quality. I predict that the slow development pace and moderate-priced housing markets of Portland will change soon to something like the frenetic Seattle and West Coast pace, but it will be handled better than anywhere else in the country.

The shift to a global "post industrial" economy is affecting cities differently. Those with a long-term corporate headquarters and "words and numbers" (information and service) industry are having an easier time adjusting than those more tied to industrial production. Those historically in the word and numbers business have also had an easier time maintaining a viable downtown.

The long-term migration of blacks to industrial cities has resulted in large concentrations of blacks in those cities now most threatened by economic restructuring. This adds a geographic dimension to the apparent disproportionate impact of economic restructuring upon minorities, particularly blacks.

While there are homeless in all of these cities, there are differences in housing policy emphasis. In the booming cities affordability gets attention. In the economically weaker cities, housing condition is more of an issue where there is a good supply of moderate-priced housing requiring considerable public input to maintain its physical condition. In some of these cities, active public programs of rehabilitation funds, low income write-downs, low interest loans, low down payments, and other housing assistance financing are literally making the market for inner city housing. This is, of course, somewhat relative, but in sharp contrast to the gentrification, increased values, and development pressures dominant in coastal cities or other economically booming places.

In every city, location and good original design combine to create persistently strong neighborhoods, able to hold economic value and sometimes, to successfully sustain racial integration: Chatham in Pittsburgh, Roland Park in Baltimore, the Magnolia area of Seattle, West Hills in Portland, the boulevards of Denver, neighborhoods north of downtown Atlanta. Good design clearly encourages good economic and social development, while its absence almost guarantees long-term economic weakness.

While the most discussed items of city government are financing and taxation, these are not as critical to future well-being as the social and physical conditions of the inner city. Finances will always be a problem, but seldom need to be a crisis. The wealth is available in the cities, metropolitan areas and states to finance city needs. Financial crises are due more to political than economic failure.

A new round of discussion about the need for metropolitan-scale governance and planning is beginning, growing mostly out of transportation and environmental concerns that have clearly become unmanageable at the local government scale. But the discussion also includes housing and social issues.

In most cases the metropolitan mechanism being discussed or put in place is statewide legislation that mandates a regional and local planning response to development, environmental, transportation, and inclusionary housing goals. The best example is Oregon, continuing a course started in the early 1970s, but Florida, Georgia, New Jersey, Vermont, and other states have also enacted strong regional planning legislation. The strong air quality regulations released for Los Angeles are apparently being taken seriously. Even

the reactive and shortsighted U.S. auto industry has so large a
market segment in Los Angeles that it is paying attention.

It is clear that the Twin Cities is no longer the national leader
in innovative regional planning. The innovation public officials in
other cities most ask about is fiscal disparities, enacted by the
Minnesota legislature fifteen years ago. Other mid-sized cities have
much stronger inclusionary housing programs. Denver has a
cooperative regional economic development marketing program,
though not in its Council of Governments, that is innovative in its
philosophy of cooperation among jurisdictions and its sophisticated
use of computer networks. Oregon's growth management program
is better than that in the Twin Cities. Florida is considering legislation that challenges the inevitability of the housing market and is
intended to shift growth from the fringe to inner city reinvestment.

The situation that reveals what is most important to the future
well-being of these cities is the extreme contrast among neighborhoods, their physical and social conditions, who lives there, and the
wide differences in fundamental livability. Though not physically
visible, the most important difference is the opportunity or probability for people to lead successful lives. The shift from the older,
resource-based economy to the new service economy is as vivid in
the cities as in smaller resource towns. In the cities it is made vivid
by contrast.

In Baltimore Harbor abandoned warehouses and factories are
intermixed with funky shops, bars and restaurants and condo-
miniums. Driving through neighborhoods occupied by people
connected to the new economy, one sees new Audi and Saab
automobiles. In the neighborhoods connected to the old economy
the autos are more likely late model American. In neighborhoods
disconnected from any economy are dilapidated cars of all makes
and sizes. In unconnected neighborhoods people are on the
sidewalks; not so in the connected places, except near the funky
shopping centers.

In Pittsburgh, near the north end of the bridge over the Monon-
gahela River, is the large Oakland community of the Carnegie
Mellon Institute, the University of Pittsburgh, Chatham College,
and a vast medical complex undergoing a $300 million expansion.
The surrounding residential areas are well-kept and prosperous, but
stressed by development pressure. On the other hand, just across the
bridge south of the river is an abandoned steel mill, the beginning
of miles of closed and rusting mills strung out along the Mon
Valley. The remaining businesses along the highway, which serves
as the main street for these towns, offer basic services and goods.
There is no apparent development pressure on these neighborhoods.

In all metropolitan cities are one or more residential areas char-
acterized by older, poorly maintained housing, predominantly low

income residents, high levels of welfare use and unemployment, high crime rates, high proportions of children living in single-parent households, and weak retail and commercial services. This is almost always within the central city and near enough to the downtown center that "inner city" is a reasonably accurate name for the place. The term "inner city," as I have said, is generally understood as not only a place, but a set of declining physical, social and economic conditions.

Failure to solve or manage inner city problems in past locations spreads these problems. Chaos and bad news from one area feed into and weaken adjacent and entire central city housing markets. It seems quite clear that early efforts meet with more success than efforts later in the decline cycle. Last-ditch efforts are almost invariably holding actions, at best.

In most cities the areas that will next be subject to neighborhood decline are quite predictable, while the success of the response is much less so. The sector theory of metropolitan development holds that the economic and social characteristics that begin in a sector of the central city will determine the characteristics of subsequent development in that same radial or pie slice sector as growth moves outward from the center. While by no means neat and precise, this does seem to happen. It can be combined with specific design and location characteristics to predict future pressures on specific neighborhoods and thus should be part of housing and development policy and planning.

When the situation has reached an advanced state of decline, it's too late for public investment in housing programs. If social conditions, public health and safety, sanitation, and education results have begun to fail, housing investment can bring limited improvement in individual shelter conditions. It will not revitalize a neighborhood. A clear distinction should be made (though it seldom is) between public housing investments for low income shelter and those intended for neighborhood revitalization. The two are quite different purposes that become muddled among housing professionals.

Contrast in opportunity is written all over city and metropolitan neighborhoods. Whatever it is in the larger system that creates poverty, the dynamics of metropolitan housing markets concentrate that poverty in inner city areas and the concentration deepens poverty.

Thinking about what is happening in these cities and metropolitan areas reconvinces one of the obvious. Our entire society is paying an enormous cost for our unfinished business of dealing with racial attitudes, past and present. Racism, of course, deprives minorities of opportunity. More specifically, racial attitudes are a major factor in metropolitan housing markets, which inexorably segregate metropolitan areas, socially and economically. This process costs everyone. Because, in part, of unresolved issues of race, we are throwing away neighborhoods and rebuilding them on the fringes at a loss to the environment, to transportation systems, to existing infrastructure, to shopping areas, farm land, and more.

Partially because of racial issues, we are abandoning existing housing and overspending on the construction of new housing, using resources and national savings that could better be used for economic growth. We are bringing school systems to their knees, enduring crime, drugs, health and social problems, all significantly related to our failure to deal with racial issues.

When these conditions are considered from a public policy viewpoint it is easy to conclude, as I have, that this inner city situation is the one that most threatens the future well-being of central cities. It is the most important development issue in metropolitan areas, including the Twin Cities. It is clear that no one has in place a comprehensive strategy likely to bring about fundamental change.

It is also clear that the underlying causes of inner city conditions do not start at city scale or end at the metropolitan level. Inner city concentrations can be found in metropolitan areas throughout the country. In most cases it became worse during the 1980s. Given the diversity among places and important differences in economics, geography, social and cultural patterns, politics and governmental structure, if the problem were caused by the city itself, there would be places where it would not occur or would have been solved. There are not.

In Atlanta, despite a very strong economy and downtown; some thriving close-in neighborhoods; booming fringe development; modern, highly affluent shopping centers; a regional rail transit system; and better than average metropolitan planning, the expected inner city concentrations of poverty are there. Downtown Atlanta seems a last outpost of the affluent society as it moves northward, away from the poor and minority areas to the south. The fortresses of this outpost are typified by Portman's architecture, protective to the point of being racist, clearly telling the "outs" to stay out.

In Cincinnati, with a strong history of reform government; a city manager government; innovative planning at least since World War II; extensive urban renewal; a quite successful, well-designed downtown; and strong neighborhood leadership, the Over-the-Rhine area continues as a very difficult inner city concentration of poverty.

In Indianapolis, the effective strong mayor form of city-county government has recreated the downtown as a regional commercial and multipurpose center, is doing impressive metropolitan planning through the combined government, continues as an important insurance center, but, as in other places, shows visible concentrations of inner city poverty.

Portland Oregon is a very livable place. It has a well-designed, pedestrian-friendly downtown; light rail transit and forward-looking transportation planning and management; the most effective metropolitan planning in the country; an effective redevelopment agency; a commission form of city government; early and effective urban renewal; and very visible homeless in the downtown, as well as concentrations of low income households, particularly in the northeast neighborhood.

Pittsburgh has mobilized leadership to clean up air pollution, to survive the loss of the steel economy and become known as a highly livable city, to redevelop downtown, to establish an aggressive city housing program, and to rebuild the airport. It has maintained some extremely vital neighborhoods and a thriving medical and education complex. It also has very visible inner city concentrations of poverty and homelessness, particularly in its Hill District.

Baltimore has in Harbor Place one of the country's most successful city redevelopment projects. While becoming the catalyst for further economic growth and redevelopment is always predicted for projects, in this case it really has occurred because of Harbor Place's unique location, economic change, and proximity to Washington, D.C. The contrasts resulting from the transition from industrial to service economy, and associated life style, are vivid in the inner city and the suburbs, as the Washington, D.C. economy spreads out into the Baltimore housing market.

Housing conditions vary enormously between low income areas of west Baltimore and the north part of the city and suburbs. Just a few blocks from Harbor Place, the city's Howard Street retail and streetscape program has not succeeded in recreating a retail market, and shows significant commercial abandonment in spite of major public investment. Its market weakness is directly tied to the large concentrations of low income residents and poverty in West Baltimore.

Seattle has a booming economy, low unemployment, a high rate of residential and commercial development, very strong central city neighborhoods, a vital downtown and waterfront, a reactivated planning function, development controversy, transportation problems and, like every city, low income neighborhoods. Seattle was an early leader in successful metropolitan approaches to urban problems, particularly water pollution, but now seems to lack organization and power at the scale needed to deal with its problems, even with a strong city mayor and executive at the county level.

Because of sound initial design, many Denver central city neighborhoods remain very desirable. This is a place where a strong mayor and other leaders are moving forward on many fronts. Innovative housing and social programs are underway. However, the Cole neighborhood, northeast of downtown, is visibly low income, and declining—the target of one of the most ambitious and innovative neighborhood revitalization programs in the country.

It is clear that inner city problems are not fundamentally caused or eliminated by city actions, governance, development policies, or short-term economic conditions. These factors affect how well the symptoms are managed, but cannot prevent the occurrence of inner city concentrations of poverty and related conditions. In spite of a diverse and variable set of economic, political and governance conditions, poverty will occur in each city. This is no surprise, but inner city problems are often debated as if they were caused only by the city and its governance. They are, in fact, caused by forces more basic and long-term and of much larger scale.

Where programs have proceeded in spite of these forces, there are some successes. Many of the social programs of the 1960s and 1970s do, in fact, work. Headstart is the most obvious. Housing assistance and social services have been combined in such places as Warren Village in Denver to point people toward successful living. Where actually carried out, subsidized housing in suburban locations has resulted in improved educational and employment success for occupants. This is verified by research discussed more in a later chapter, but it is a premise of this report that low income people do share the larger societal values about work and education and housing. When something happens to change the negative inertia of a situation, their shared values can bear fruit.

It is also my belief that we do, in fact, know a great deal about what works, about what specific programs can improve specific social and inner city problems. What we seem not to know is how to deploy that knowledge at the scale of the problem; how to do several coordinated, supportive things at once; or how to agree upon and put in place a comprehensive strategy that gets at permanent, fundamental improvement.

Conclusions

There is a tendency for those who can move to move away from those who can't. Racial attitudes and economic class are deeply involved in this tendency and metropolitan housing markets provide the means for this tendency to become residential practice and geography. Those who can leave really don't want those unlike them, in economic and social status and race, to follow. Those who can't leave are left behind and become the inner city.

After enough observation and thought, the obvious finally becomes obvious. Low income people and poverty conditions are concentrated in inner city areas because that is where we want them to be. It is, in fact, our national belief, translated into metropolitan housing policy, that this is where they are supposed to be. Additionally, they are to have as little presence as possible elsewhere in the metropolitan area.

It is only a slight overstatement to suggest that an unspoken agreement has been struck between the city and suburbs. Suburban communities don't want poor people, and in some ways the central cities need the needy. The poor don't fit the image of the suburban good life with its neighborhoods, schools, parks, shopping centers and jobs. The cities need them to occupy housing and neighborhoods that the more affluent market has rejected, as statistics to make the case for special funding consideration from higher levels of government, as voters, as clients for the public and nonprofit social service and housing bureaucracy and system. Cities need their housing assistance as a source of financing, and as occupants for redevelopment areas.

Consequently, there is almost no discussion about changing, or effort to fundamentally change the situation. Low income people are to be concentrated in the inner portion of the central city. Cheap shelter is to be mostly created by the devaluation of inner city neighborhoods. Others will send some money, and the central cities will try to respond to the resulting social, economic and service difficulties.

This arrangement works, sort of. But conflicts arise. More low income people need more low income housing. Residents of stable or declining areas try to hold together the social and marketplace strength of their neighborhoods. Public policy ignores the fundamental conflict between these two needs. One area gets renewed or revitalized, nice annual reports show projects and progress every year, people get pushed somewhere else, and another neighborhood declines.

This is one reason why after decades of work to revitalize neighborhoods, most cities have more areas in difficulty than before the work began. Such revitalization is in direct conflict with our national housing policy of devitalization as a means of providing low income shelter.

Another conflict arises when the inner city becomes not only the recipient of low income households and poverty, but when the resulting isolation and concentration become the causes of further poverty; when the quality of basic city services sinks so low that residents are deprived of basic public safety, public health, supportive neighborhood surroundings, and sufficient education to prepare them for economic opportunity. At that point, the societal policy about where low income people will live becomes debilitating, life-threatening and, we hope, unacceptable in a democratic society.

I started by asking what in our present central city situation is most threatening to our long-term well-being. The answer is clearly our inner city situation—the social, economic, and physical conditions in some primarily residential areas of the inner part of the central cities. No other situation is so damaging to human well-being, so threatens overall city viability, or pervades other city issues. This inner city situation is not only the most important city issue, it is the most important development issue in Minneapolis-St. Paul, and most other metropolitan areas.

This is not a surprising conclusion. I would like to have concluded that we already have a solution, or that with time the inner city problem will go away. It would also have been comforting to conclude that there is a single answer to the inner city problem, such as housing, or getting rid of drugs, or law enforcement or family rehabilitation. There is not.

A complex, multilevel approach that gets closer to basic causes is needed. The rest of this report is an attempt to develop such a strategy. The next chapter examines to what extent these conditions do indeed occur in the Twin Cities, traces trends and causes, and sets the stage for the strategy discussions.

Chapter Two

How Market and Public Policy Forces Create Inner City Conditions

> This combination of concentration and mixture, with isolation and differentiation, is one of the characteristic marks of the new urban culture. On the positive side there was friendly cohabitation, spiritual communion, wide communication, and a complex system of vocational co-operation. But on the negative side, the citadel introduced class segregation, unfeelingness and irresponsiveness, secrecy, authoritarian control, and ultimate violence.
>
> Lewis Mumford, 1961, p. 47.

While this report deals mostly with the post-1950 period, the tendency for cities to divide along economic class and ethnic lines is historical. Sam Bass Warner, in "A Selective Melting Pot," in his book *Streetcar Suburbs, The Process of Growth, 1870-1900* notes that in Boston, "by 1900 the interaction of the growth of the street railway and class building patterns had produced class-segregated suburbs. As the bands of new construction moved ever outward, they impressed upon the land their own special architectural and social patterns" (p. 64).

In *The Twin Cities of Minneapolis and St. Paul* the authors follow development trends from initial settlement to 1970 and note class separation early in development. "Before 1900, neighborhood quality generally rose with increasing distance from industry, railroad yards, and the downtown. Congestion, high densities, and general squalor near the mills gradually gave way to lower densities, higher ground, and cleaner air farther away. At the same time that St. Paul's upper class selected the bluffs west of downtown as the place to live, they assigned to railroads and industry increasing amounts of land east and north of downtown where railroads con-

verged. The same thing happened in Minneapolis. Much East Side
land and parcels along the river on the West Side were devoted to
railroads and industry as the upper class moved into South and
Southwest Minneapolis" (Abler, Adams and Borchert, 22).

In *Where We Live, The Residential Districts of Minneapolis
and St. Paul*, the authors also describe very early tendencies toward
ethnic segregation. "It was a commonly accepted view of the late
nineteenth and early twentieth century urban life that each ethnic
group sought to inhabit a distinct section of the inner city. As these
groups prospered and became Americanized, they and their off-
spring moved outward toward the edges of the city and mixed with
other ethnic groups" (Martin and Lanegran, 6).

While these patterns and tendencies are long-standing,
accelerated and somewhat different patterns began to emerge about
1950. Figure 1 shows the Twin Cities metropolitan and central city
population from 1850 to 1990. The central city population peaked
about 1950, with St. Paul holding longer near its peak population
because of more undeveloped land within its limits. The peak is
first explained more by a growing population creating a housing
demand and market response that encountered fixed municipal
boundaries than by such phenomena as "white flight" or strong
desire to live outside of the central cities. People went where housing could be built. In some metropolitan areas where central city
boundaries did expand, there are still inner area social and
economic problems. However, in the Twin Cities, as in most metropolitan areas, being outside of the central city did eventually
become part of the housing market equation as inner city conditions
were inaccurately defined as representing the entire central city. In
this report, as I have pointed out, "central city" and "inner city" are
not interchangeable terms.

While the mid-century peaking of central city population is
explained largely by saturation of available land, the subsequent
decline in population is explained primarily by smaller families and
households. The decline in family size also occurred in suburbs
after the advent of effective birth control in about 1960, but there
the decline in family size was overwhelmingly counteracted by the
large number of housing units being constructed. The more or less
fixed number of units in the cities housed fewer people as families
became smaller and as fewer units housed families.

Figure 1. Twin Cities Population Growth, 1850 to 1990

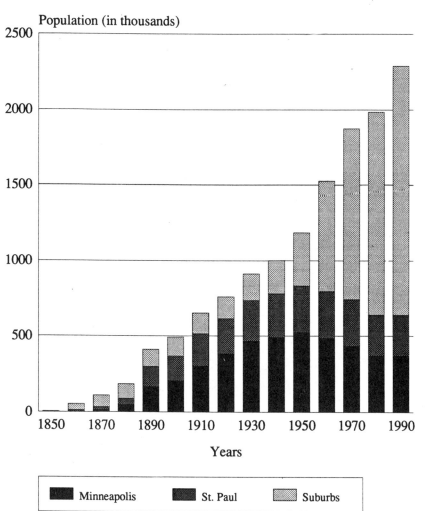

As the housing market after World War II accelerated, it became a more potent agent of change. More housing was constructed and people moved more within the existing stock. Millions of residential location changes contributed to the increasing separation of economic classes. Cumulatively, these moves created today's economic and ethnic distribution of population. The housing market is large and active enough to carry out the tendency of people to socially and economically segregate. This tendency was reinforced as neighborhoods and entire cities were assigned a status or reputation, and as self-reinforcing prophecy gave the reputation some element of accuracy.

Figure 2.   How the Development Process Created Decline in the Twin Cities, 1950 to 1990

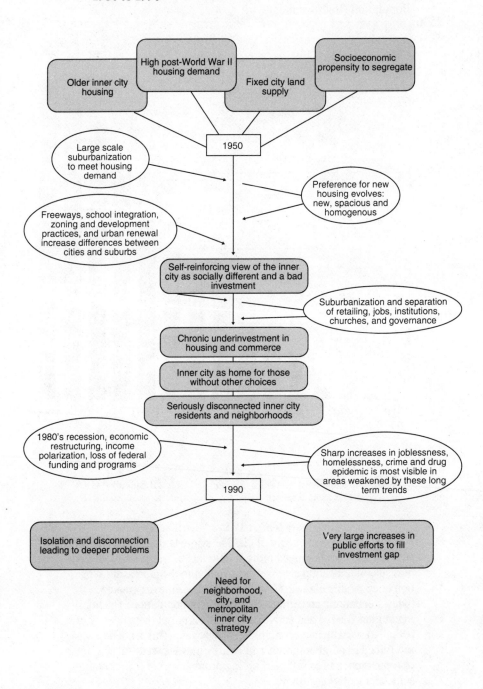

Figure 2 illustrates the interaction among the most important aspects of the 1950-1990 process. It is not possible to say exactly what happened first, and there is complex interaction and feedback among causes. Thus, only in an approximate way does this chart represent the sequence of change or the relative importance of the factors.

Beginning in the 1950s, families who could do so were locating in the suburbs, initially because that's where the housing they wanted was located. In addition to and before concerns about schools, crime, services and social conditions, many families were choosing the new, modern house with a double garage, multiple bathrooms, larger yard, and homogeneity available in the suburbs. Highway improvements were making the suburbs increasingly accessible. Where these features were available in the central cities outside of the inner city, housing was and is highly marketable. Where such features do not exist, older housing is at a disadvantage, even without underlying social and neighborhood issues.

In some neighborhoods, changes in ownership and occupancy become a pattern of transfer from those with more to those with less. Problems begin to surface as deteriorating housing, caused by chronic under-investment in maintenance and little new construction. Housing becomes owned and/or occupied by people who cannot or choose not to invest enough to maintain property at a level that keeps it viable in the profit marketplace, or eventually, to meet public standards. Research shows that housing expenditures are not income elastic among low income, that is, an increase in income is unlikely to be spent on housing. This is understandable, given other needs and the high portion of income already being spent on basic shelter. Thus, chronic under-investment is inevitable (Bourne, 130).

The decline in value and eventual decline in condition is the principal means by which our de facto national housing policy provides shelter for low income people. Side effects of a number of otherwise useful and necessary public policies and programs began to complicate the situation by making the inner city increasingly different from the rest of the region. Among these were transportation changes—including construction of the freeway system, zoning and development practices; the decisions that the most pro-active racial integration efforts would be in schools at the district level rather than in the housing market at the metropolitan scale; inadequate response to increasingly difficult educational challenges; and construction of most public housing as large homogeneous projects in already low income areas, because of the political difficulty of putting it anywhere else.

While legislated national housing policy since 1949 has been safe and sanitary housing for everyone, the most powerful federal program has encouraged ownership of housing and construction of new housing for middle and upper income people, and reduced its cost by allowing mortgage interest as an income tax deduction. Early in this period federal mortgage guarantee review procedures encouraged or required homogeneity of race and income in new development, and continues to in some aspects.

Describing the period between 1957 and 1971, Abler, Adams and Borchert note "The Jewish departure from the Minneapolis, Near North left vacant many quality houses which were promptly occupied by black families. Prosperity encouraged the better-off and upwardly mobile black families to move westward and north-ward away from the North Side ghetto core near 6th Avenue North and Lyndale. As they moved, others followed, pushed along by urban renewal projects" (p. 24).

Low income housing was to be provided by moving low income people into the housing middle and upper income people moved out of. This filtering process not only reinforces the segregationist tendencies of the housing market, but requires a surplus of housing in order to take place. Some housing abandonment must occur, which further destroys neighborhood conditions for those left behind.

Generally, this federal housing policy must inevitably cause the decline of inner cities as a place to live and reinforce the differences between those who live there and those who live elsewhere. This housing policy cannot be counteracted by open housing laws and half-hearted efforts to place lower-priced housing in the suburbs. In the Twin Cities, about 20,000 units of subsidized housing are located in suburbs, compared to 500,000 units of market rate housing added since 1950.

This was further aggravated by zoning ordinances requiring minimum lot and house sizes, which encouraged economic segregation. The 1970s saw the adoption of more flexible ordinances in some communities, but the housing that preceded these changes remains generally unavailable for moderate and low income persons.

The housing market was supported by other systems. The transportation system has undergone great change since 1950. The streetcar system was removed in favor of the bus, the transit vehicle preferred by automobile manufacturers. The freeway system was undertaken in the 1960s. Automobiles came into their own. Metropolitan-wide mobility by other than automobile became increasingly difficult. Those unable to own and maintain a reliable automobile were seriously handicapped, were unable, in fact, to interact with the larger community.

The freeway system, as had the streetcar system earlier, contributed to the economic sorting and segregation of households.

While enhancing downtown growth, the radial nature of streetcars and freeways reduced the relative competitiveness of city neighborhoods in the housing market, and made it more possible to work in the center and live outward. Later in the development process jobs followed, probably resulting from both new residential locations and highways. This began the process of separating some jobs from lower income housing. The other side of this picture is that by making continued downtown growth possible, some service jobs were kept in the city near low income residential areas.

The question is not whether the freeway system should have been built. It is one of several cases where an otherwise useful and probably necessary public action has a side effect—a cause of current disconnection and social isolation. In sum, these public actions have contributed significantly to the problem. Thus it is logical that we seek a public solution at the same scale. In transportation, the impact upon the inner city should be thought about in the location, phasing, and setting of priorities for future transportation improvements, including the proposed light rail system.

Since 1954, public education systems have worked to comply with school desegregation decisions. During the same general period, housing integration decisions and legislation have been much less pro-active. Might thirty-five years of comparable effort applied to the housing market have achieved better results?

The necessary deemphasis of neighborhood schools to achieve racial balance, the inevitable controversy, the uncertainty about outcomes, all reinforced the difference between city and suburb in the metropolitan housing market. Because desegregation occurred in schools rather than in housing and because it was implemented only in the city rather than metropolitan-wide, a new force for economic separation was introduced into the metropolitan housing market.

Metropolitan programs in the 1960s and 1970s to resolve serious pollution problems by extension of sewers to large new development areas loosened up the housing market even more and further contributed to economic and social separation. The 1970s metropolitan plan to contain future urban density development within an urban service area may have begun to slow this separation. But it was specifically designed not to constrain the housing market, except in rural areas. That effort was the first step, i.e., when you have dug yourself into a hole, the first thing to do is to stop digging. The definition and legislation of a metropolitan urban service area in the 1970s represented a decision to stop digging ourselves into the hole, but it's not enough.

As the housing development process played out, other elements had to follow housing location. Retailing, as it expanded with the growing market, also took on the new form of regional shopping malls. Industrial expansion took on a new form of horizontal, single-floor structures on expansive land parcels not generally available in the inner city. While the housing market was forcing some to stay behind, industrial change was forcing the new jobs to move away, beginning the separation of jobs from the inner city that is an important piece of the present dilemma. Churches, though there are very important exceptions, had to move away completely or divide into an inner city and suburban congregation. Dozens of full-fledged municipal governments had to form to provide needed services. All of these changes contributed to the social and economic separation of the population.

To list these effects is not to second guess, but to again say that accumulated results of public decisions have created situations that need continued public attention. Perhaps we find ourselves in the turbulent middle of a rather wide stream originally deemed worth crossing. We need to finish the journey before we capsize or make the mistake of thinking that we can turn back.

A way to look at this process of change is to select areas that represent different conditions and to trace the growth of that difference (Figure 3). This was done for two clusters of low income census tracts—one cluster in St. Paul and the other in Minneapolis. Also traced was the cluster of high income suburban census tracts that make up the present city of Edina. The low income clusters were among the Twin Cities' lowest income areas and the high income area was near the highest in the 1980 census.

The analysis of these areas, relative to one another and to the metropolitan area, shows that the long-term development process continuously sorted households into increasingly different kinds of places from 1950 to 1980. This process set the stage for the intense inner city problems of the 1980s and those that can be expected in the 1990s.

The low income areas were depopulating while others were developing. The Minneapolis low income tracts depopulated from 56,900 people to 22,700 and the St. Paul low income tracts from 30,600 to 15,900, while the suburban area developed from 9,700 to 46,000 people.

The suburban area was typified by home ownership. The low income tracts changed increasingly to rental housing and to public housing.

In 1950 the median income of the high income tracts was 2.5 times that of the Minneapolis tracts. By 1980 it was 5.8 times larger. Income in the low income areas grew less rapidly than in the metropolitan area as a whole. In the high income area income grew more rapidly than the metropolitan area.

All areas showed increases in minority population: the suburban section from .2 to 1.6 percent, representing several hundred people (p. 740), the Minneapolis tracts from 6.9 to 38.9 percent

(8,822 people), and the St. Paul tracts from 7.3 to 35.5 percent (5,637 people).

Sawhill and Hughes, researchers on inner city and poverty issues, suggest statistical measures which they believe portray accurately, in a behavioral and causal way, the severity of conditions in low income areas. The measures used are welfare dependency, adult male joblessness, single-parent households, and premature school leaving. High levels of these measures describe the most severe conditions of concentration and isolation in areas they call "impacted ghettos." These exact variables cannot be traced well over the long term and the Twin Cities do not have large areas that would be described as "impacted ghettos." There are, however, clear trends as shown in Figure 4.

Metropolitan wide, and in high income tracts, the trend in proportion of working adult males between 16 and 65 was quite stable, but it shows a steady, gradual decline in the low income areas. A number of demographic and development factors could contribute to this trend and more specific analyses are needed. Chapter Five shows that some researchers place considerable importance upon adult male joblessness as a fundamental cause of single-parent households and resulting poverty problems.

The numbers of children living in single-parent households have been increasing for a long time, but have only recently begun to receive attention. Figure 4 shows that single-parent households increased throughout the metro area, but became the normal situation in low income areas.

In these inner city census tracts, education levels of adult residents were low, though rising, while relative income was declining. Because the analysis deals with averages, one cannot quite conclude that in this inner city area increased education is associated with less income. The averages may have been skewed by trends in a small portion of the area. However these areas did not, prior to 1980, exhibit the increased proportion of adult residents who had left school prematurely that might be predicted from income trends. The area seems to house people who have shared in the national trend of increasing education achievement, but not in rising income levels. It suggests that a complex set of trends are emerging as population turns over and the social and economic sorting processes play out.

The data just presented are about fixed areas and how they changed relative to each other and to the metropolitan area. It is arithmetically and logically possible that this data represents spatial relocation of existing societal conditions rather than increasing concentration. This would not change the basic premise about the creation of inner city conditions, but might lead to different conclusions about remedies.

Figure 3. Development Trends in High and Low Income Areas of the Twin Cities

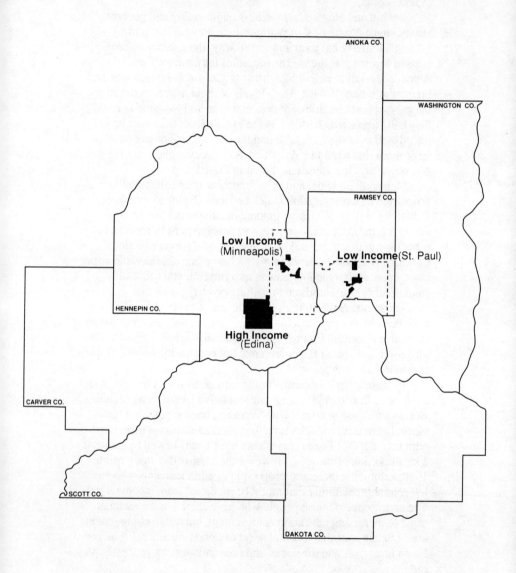

Figure 3. continued

Low Income Census Tracts (Minneapolis)

	1950	1960	1970	1980
Population	56,900	40,600	25,700	22,700
Average median income	$2,300	$2,900	$3,300	$5,800
Percent minority population	6.9	14.3	24.1	38.9
Percent owner-occupied housing	15.8	11.2	6.4	6.3

Low Income Census Tracts (St. Paul)

	1950	1960	1970	1980
Population	30,600	25,600	16,800	15,900
Average median income	$2,700	$3,700	$4,100	$8,900
Percent minority population	7.3	11.4	15.2	35.5
Percent owner-occupied housing	27.6	28.5	22.6	27.0

High Income Census Tracts (Edina)

	1950	1960	1970	1980
Population	9,700	28,500	44,000	46,000
Average median income	$5,700	$11,700	$17,600	$33,700
Percent minority population	0.2	0.2	0.3	1.6
Percent owner-occupied housing	87.3	91.2	80.3	73.2

Entire Metropolitan Area

	1950	1960	1970	1980
Population	1,186,000	1,525,000	1,874,000	1,986,000
Average median income	3,800	6,800	11,700	24,600
Percent minority population	1.3	1.7	2.6	5.0
Percent owner-occupied housing	60.3	68.2	65.2	67.0

Figure 4. Trends in Social Indicators for High and Low Income Areas (in percents)

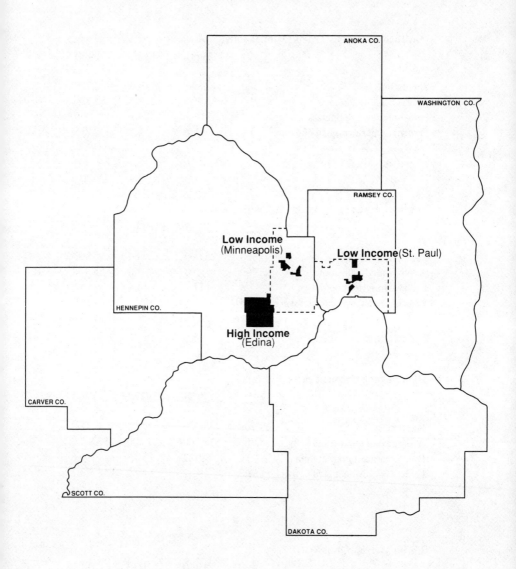

Figure 4. continued

Low Income Census Tracts (Minneapolis)

	1960	1970	1980
Adult male work force participation	71.3	59.2	55.5
Children in single-parent homes	25.6	48.8	66.4
High school graduates in population	30.3	36.9	57.2
College graduates in population	3.8	4.7	14.0

Low Income Census Tracts (St. Paul)

	1960	1970	1980
Adult male work force participation	74.0	66.0	60.0
Children in single-parent homes	22.2	38.5	51.0
High school graduates in population	26.4	34.5	53.4
College graduates in population	2.8	3.7	9.9

High Income Census Tracts (Edina)

	1960	1970	1980
Adult male work force participation	80.6	83.1	81.3
Children in single-parent homes	2.9	4.4	10.8
High school graduates in population	82.0	89.0	93.0
College graduates in population	27.9	36.2	44.6

Entire Metropolitan Area

	1960	1970	1980
Adult male work force participation	83.4	81.7	81.5
Children in single-parent homes	7.8	8.8	14.9
High school graduates in population	52.6	66.1	79.9
College graduates in population	10.4	14.8	21.9

One could use a different approach. Rather than using the same geographic areas, the analysis could float to wherever the most extreme conditions occurred. That approach shows that the median metropolitan income increased from $3,776 in 1950 to $20,699 in 1980. In 1950, the average median income of the three lowest income census tracts in the Twin Cities was $996, or 26 percent of the metropolitan median. In 1980, the average median income of the three lowest income tracts in the Twin Cities, not the same three as in 1950, was $4,781, or 23 percent of the metropolitan median. The metropolitan area was more polarized by income in 1980 than in 1950.

While a more sophisticated economic segregation analysis may be useful, Figures 3 and 4 clearly show that at the extremes the metropolitan area has, for a long time, been separating itself into different kinds of places, different kinds of people, different housing markets. Moreover, early separation has reinforced subsequent disconnection.

Even if there had been a metropolitan municipality rather than central cities surrounded by suburbs, inner city conditions would occur somewhere as those with low income sought shelter in the cheapest housing in the market. However, boundaries probably reinforce concentration of conditions and will be discussed more later.

From 1950 to 1980, a great deal of effort and progress was made in civil rights, affirmative action, national and metropolitan economic growth, housing and social programs, and regional planning. Yet economic segregation increased. These social programs were simply no match for the strength of the development process, the housing market dynamics, and a variety of public policies and actions working toward separation.

Why is it that in the late 1970s and in the 1980s, inner city conditions began to decline at what appears to be an even more rapid rate? Why, given the previous effort by cities to stabilize the housing stock, metropolitan planning, civil rights and affirmative action programs, the great society and the war on poverty and the general though inaccurate perception that city problems were solved in the 1970s, do things seem now to be worse than ever?

That the inner city did deteriorate in the 1980s is verified by statistics about Minneapolis prepared for the 1989 Comprehensive Law Enforcement Plan (Comprehensive Law Enforcement Plan, Minneapolis City Planning Department, November, 1989). The number of mothers receiving inadequate prenatal care increased from 6.1 percent in 1980 to 9.7 percent in 1987. Infant mortality rates, which had dropped from 21.8 per 1,000 live births in 1970 to 9.2 in 1985, began to increase, reaching 12.7 in 1987. Reported personal crimes (homicide, rape, robbery, assault) increased from 11,500 in 1983 to 21,400 in 1988 and continued to be concentrated in the inner city. Homicide rates in Minneapolis remain well below those in many cities and fluctuate a lot from year to year, but definitely increased from 1980 to 1988. Property damage crimes increased from 5,800 to 8,550 from 1983 to 1988. All of these increases were, as with the media-noted drug crime increases, primarily inner city rather than central city phenomena.

What happened? First, political proclamations notwithstanding, urban problems were not solved, nor did they go away in the 1970s. The long-range social trends never changed, but were dampened and covered by an apparently strong national economy, by downtown revitalization success, and by a lot of useful public and private investment in the physical conditions of housing and neighborhoods. But as the long-term social isolation continued, the stage was set for several national trends to play out vividly in inner city neighborhoods weakened by the long-range trends discussed above.

The national economy was and is undergoing structural change, reducing the growth and pay scale of lower skilled jobs. More such jobs are ending up paying less and located in the suburbs—less accessible and less remunerative to lower income residential areas. The new better paying jobs are less available to those without fuller education, training and metropolitan scale proximity or transportation. This is basically the William Julius Wilson thesis discussed in later chapters. If Wilson is right, those cities more fitted to the new economy and less tied to the resource economy are somewhat spared, but would logically become the destination for emigration from those cities more directly damaged.

Second, the 1980s began with a severe recession that aggravated the effect of economic restructuring. Some jobs just didn't come back. Some people never got to begin to work.

Third, high unemployment was accepted as the justified cost of controlling the very high inflation rate of the early 1980s.

Fourth, the 1980s reduction in federal programs and funding began to reduce effective income and services for low income areas and neighborhoods. Also, at the urging of our political leaders, we decided that it was necessary, in the age of computers, to simplify the income tax system. In the process, we eliminated a great deal of progressivity. The redistributive effect of the federal government was reduced by both the tax and program changes, contributing further to the income polarization brought about by the economic restructuring. All of this contributed to joblessness, homelessness, and general economic isolation that focused upon the people and neighborhoods left vulnerable by the longer-range trends we have been discussing.

These long-term trends, and the 1980s, have created extreme social isolation and disconnection. The conditions of these neighborhoods, and the resulting social isolation, are the result of larger social problems. The resulting isolation and absence of life chances is debilitating not only to the individuals, families and neighborhoods directly involved, but to our entire society and economy. This is the most important development issue facing the Twin Cities.

Notwithstanding decades of frequently successful federal, state, metropolitan and city efforts, economic cycles, and pronouncements that the problems have been solved, the answers to basic questions tell another story: "How are the people doing?" and "How is it as a place to live?" elicit the following, "Not quite as well as last year." "A little worse than in the 1970s." "A lot better than Detroit or Cleveland, but slipping some."

If long-term trends get a little worse every year for a long enough time, eventually things will be pretty bad. If, on the other hand, the same trends would get a little better every year, the difference in a decade or two would be significant.

While New York City was not part of this study, it could be used to make two points. First, alongside of great and apparently continuing economic success and cultural power, it is possible for large portions of a city to fail as a place for people to live, to become a place where public services such as sanitation, safety and education for large areas and many people have deteriorated beyond recovery.

The other point about New York City is that it still is thriving in many ways. While a national and world economic center may be able to go on economically in spite of continued social decline— sort of high rise above it all—most cities are not well enough positioned in the national and global economy, or sufficiently exciting and stimulating, to continue economic success in association with anywhere near that degree of loss of livability and municipal function. The Twin Cities, nor other smaller metropolitan areas, should not and cannot accept anywhere near that level of decline, from either an economic or societal viewpoint.

Conclusions

To a significant degree, public policy action at all levels has had the unintended side effect of reinforcing and deepening the concentration and isolation of inner city people, families, and neighborhoods. The resulting inner city poverty has not been caused by the poor. Fixing it is not their responsibility, nor the responsibility of the central cities. Most levels of government and segments of society are part of the problem. We all suffer from it. We all should participate in the solution.

The most important factors in the inner city and neighborhood cycles of decline can be logically arranged in a sequence, a predictable "formula," that can show us how to proceed. Poverty and associated inner city problems *occur* in neighborhoods and households, but are *caused* by markets, policies and forces *much larger* than the neighborhood itself. Societal and metropolitan poverty is *concentrated* in the city by the metropolitan housing market, resulting in *isolation and disconnection* of households and neighborhoods from the metropolitan economy and opportunity. More difficult conditions lead to decline and *failure of community and public services* and *spread* into and weaken adjacent and other central city neighborhoods. The larger community denies these problems, or dissociates itself from them.

Poverty

Our socioeconomic system produces large numbers of low income individuals and households unable, or unprepared, to "do well" in the larger society and economy, some due to short-term circumstances and others in a quite permanent way.

Inner city conditions are first of all a people situation, closely related to low income and poverty—a result of poverty and a cause of poverty. Because of the concentration effect of the housing market, if national, state, and metropolitan poverty and income polarization increase, inner city difficulties will deepen and spread to more of the city. If the incidence of poverty decreases, inner city difficulties can improve.

Concentration

The metropolitan housing market does not cause poverty conditions; it does concentrate poverty into inner city conditions. That concentration leads to further poverty. The inner city typically contains concentrations of older and perhaps marketplace obsolete housing that is relatively cheap to own or occupy. Poor people must live in cheap housing, therefore they tend to locate in this inner city housing. New housing is almost never cheap housing, except when publicly assisted and then it is usually in the same areas as the old cheap housing and contributes to the concentration.

Race is clearly a factor in these trends. Whether causes are predominantly economic as the result of historic racism, or contemporary racism, or more subtle racial attitudes about where minorities "should" live, race must be considered. The metropolitan housing market is not a cause of racism, but it has encouraged racism.

People who economically can, have a strong propensity to socially and economically segregate themselves. This impulse is sometimes economic, sometimes racial, sometimes connected to financial and household security, sometimes noble and sometimes ignoble. The metropolitan housing market provides the mechanism to turn this propensity into reality. Whether or not low income households (often minority households) want it that way, and they probably don't, they have little choice but to remain behind.

All of these factors form our de facto societal, national, and metropolitan housing policy that low income shelter will be provided primarily by the devaluation of inner city neighborhoods and low income people will have as little presence as possible in other areas. This powerful force overwhelms most inner city neighborhood revitalization efforts and spreads the area of poverty within the inner city.

Housing turnover is predominantly from those with more to those with fewer resources. Add to this an increasing gap in physical maintenance, high incidence of social problems, and an increasingly difficult and less successful service delivery system and the self-fulfilling prophecies in the housing market and real estate industry are fullfilled.

Revitalization and renewal efforts that seek to restore these areas are really efforts to create a situation in which ownership and occupancy turnover consists of transfers from those with less to those with more resources—abruptly in the case of renewal, more gradually in the case of revitalization. This usually does not succeed because it is in direct conflict with the need for low income housing and with the de facto national and metropolitan housing policy. When revitalization efforts do succeed, the same situations force a neighborhood into decline somewhere else, unless balanced by large amounts of housing assistance financing.

Decline of Community, Community Services, Livability and Human Development Qualities

As the neighborhood becomes isolated from the larger society, individuals within the neighborhood become more isolated. As the troubled and troublesome concentrate in low income areas, there is a more urgent need, but less ability and expectation for public services to maintain an acceptable level of public safety, public health, education, and general neighborhood conditions.

This pervasive decline of service expectations and results is clearly a path that cities follow to failure. This community and service dilemma interacts with the social conditions to bring about the cyclical decline that eventually creates places that are human development ghettos, where the problems brought to the place are further aggravated by the place, and the neighborhood and service conditions become a cause of further poverty.

Spread and Weakening of Adjacent Neighborhoods and Entire Central Cities in the Metropolitan Housing Market

As the social, community and service conditions of the most difficult neighborhoods become known or exaggerated in the marketplace, and as more low income housing is needed and not otherwise provided, nearby areas inevitably weaken. This is also cyclical since image affects behavior and prophecies of decline become self-fulfilling. Both image and prophecy become fact.

The quality of the product being offered the metropolitan marketplace does indeed decline. Most of the information in the marketplace becomes tenuous and negative. Financing becomes more difficult and less available. All the factors for cyclical weakening are then in place.

Metropolitan Isolation and Disconnection

The tendency of the housing market to bring about socioeconomic separation results in isolation of households and neighborhoods from the larger metropolitan economy and opportunity. This is reinforced by public policy and actions in education, transportation, housing finance, public housing, redevelopment, development policy and regulation, and social service delivery systems. The isolation is also reinforced by private decisions and changes in retailing, job locations, churches and other institutions that follow and then reinforce the housing market patterns.

In response, a set of human and housing service delivery mechanisms are set up that begin to need the concentration as a market for their services, i.e., low income residents and housing subsidies as a market for redevelopment projects. This all becomes a complex set of self-reinforcing conditions and self-fulfilling prophecies in private market and public decisions about development, housing, jobs, investments, transportation, public services and facilities, and social services.

The economy, job locations, transportation, retailing, and housing markets change and move about while inner city people and places get disconnected from these changes. This is spatial isolation and transportation disconnection, but also a socioeconomic disconnection from opportunity. Eventually the social isolation from jobs and opportunity, and the concentration of problems, deepen the original problem.

Disassociation from the Situation by the Larger City, the Metropolitan Area and Society in General

Even though the underlying causes of inner city and poverty conditions are national, societal, and rooted in metropolitan development processes, there is a tendency to blame individuals, ethnic groups, and central city governance. Even those who are quite interested in general social well-being easily disassociate themselves from inner city issues, feeling no responsibility and seeing no direct consequences.

Figure 5 is a graphic illustration of the widening cycle of poverty, concentration, isolation, decline, and disassociation. (Call it the human development model of inner city decline. It is simple enough to be understood and accurate enough to be useful.)

A strategy to improve inner city conditions and prevent their reoccurrence would need to intervene in each of the factors in a human development model. It would need to switch off the connections between the factors. It would need to look at the causes of poverty and also intervene in the market and policies that concentrate that poverty. It would need to prevent remaining concentrations from diminishing human development. It would need to prevent poverty's spread to other neighborhoods. It would need to change the isolation of existing areas. It would need to work to reassociate the larger community with the situation through some combination of logic, conscience, fear and enlightened self-interest.

To improve inner city conditions a city must have both a neighborhood and metropolitan strategy, as well as a clear and active state and national agenda. The strategy would have to be patient and long-term, working to reverse the situation from slow, incremental, long-term decline to slow, incremental, long-term improvement. The central city and close-in suburbs would have to be the principal designers and advocates, though it would be very much a metropolitan strategy with a strong potential role for metropolitan agencies, as well as suburban, state and federal support.

The next chapter examines further the nature of the strategy needed; it lays out the six major components of such a strategy. Each succeeding chapter deals with one of those components in greater detail. This includes chapters on poverty reduction, improving the human development characteristics of low income areas, metropolitan housing policy to intervene in poverty concentration by the housing market, strengthening central city neighborhoods in the metropolitan housing market, metropolitan development and transportation planning to reconnect the inner city, and developing unified metropolitan leadership.

Figure 5. Path of Decline for Inner Cities

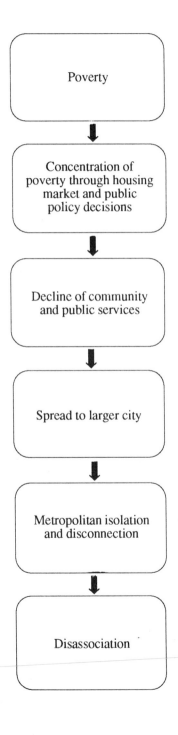

Chapter Three

Components of a City and Metropolitan Inner City Strategy

> There is much more to development than
> economics. There are cultural and social institu-
> tions, for instance.
>
> Peter F. Drucker, 1968, p. 132.

In 1988, Dr. George Sternlieb of Rutgers University, a national
scholar and expert on housing and urban development, told Minneapolis city officials that if any metropolitan area could solve its
inner city problems it would be the Twin Cities, because our
problems seem more manageable than in many other places and
also because of our tradition of innovative public problem-solving
and action.

The purpose of this section is to consider whether a strategy
could be put in place that would bring about long-term and permanent improvements in our inner cities, and to consider and
propose the major elements of such a strategy. Could Minnesota
and the Twin Cities be the place that has the brainpower, leadership
and resources to figure out how to do it and then do it?

This would require a general consensus that there is a problem
even more difficult and fundamental than the current crime, drugs,
and homelessness. It would require consensus on the nature and
magnitude of that problem and a belief that inner city conditions are
not inevitable or "natural" urban phenomena in a capitalistic
economy. It would also require consensus among city, state, and
metropolitan leadership about a shared responsibility for a strategy
of improvement. It would then be necessary to apportion responsibility for putting in place the pieces of a specific action program
that matches the scale of the problem.

This would mean not only addressing the problems that result
from the present isolation and disconnection of inner city people
and neighborhoods, but changing the systems that keep reinforcing
that concentration and isolation. We must also consider metropolitan social and economic integration; the dynamics of the

metropolitan housing market; the effect of living in low income areas upon life chances; location of and access to transportation, jobs and opportunity. Fundamental inner city issues need the serious, long-term attention the drug problem has been getting for the last decade. This means finding and applying neighborhood solutions, but also reducing the metropolitan-scale forces that deepen neighborhood problems.

This strategy would not eliminate inner city problems this year, or this term, or even this decade. But it might reverse the present situation in which conditions are slowly, steadily getting worse. It might begin long-term improvement, and sustain that improvement. By the end of the 1990s, several years of turn-around should put us in a significantly better situation. The forces, systems and programs for long-term continuation of the upward trend should be well-established.

Certainly, reaching public consensus on such knotty problems calls for ideas, analysis, and political debate. One approach is to throw up one's hands and say there will always be poor people; it is the role of the central cities to house them in the inner cities.

A step forward is to accept the inevitability of the inner city condition, but to recognize that the causes are much broader than the cities and that the larger society should at least send money to help manage the problem. This is more or less where we are, or were before the 1980s, though the amount of money sent was not deemed adequate by most advocates.

A more ambitious strategy would be to try to fundamentally change the situation. The point of view of the remainder of this report is that such a strategy could be put in place, that it would make a difference, that it must be at least metropolitan in scale, and that it must have several components, because there is no one answer.

Earlier work done in the Twin Cities gives us a modest start. Let us first quickly review some of that work.

Previous Metropolitan Planning

During the 1960s and 1970s the Twin Cities developed some good regional plans and planning processes that were national state-of-the-art. As a result of this work, groundwater pollution problems were resolved, transportation decisions got made, some suburban low income housing was developed, a regional development policy was prepared and adopted, an integrated intergovernmental planning process for development and supporting facilities was legislated and implemented, and a farsighted county and metro-politan park reserve system was put in place.

From health planning to interchange spacing on freeways, plans and programs that have made a difference were put in place by state, local, and metropolitan government.

The development planning done was primarily to manage sprawling growth in order to reduce environmental damage and farmland loss, and to get control of the costs of extending services to unplanned development.

A metropolitan problem not corrected by this work was the declining condition of our inner cities. Though given some attention, no comprehensive strategies powerful enough to reverse inner city housing, social and economic trends were put in place. Naftalin and Brandl have evaluated the work done by the Metropolitan Council from 1967 to 1980 (*The Twin Cities Regional Strategy*, Metropolitan Council, Arthur Naftalin and John Brandl, 1980). That was the development period of the strategy now in place, the 1980s being a period of refinement and implementation rather than major new strategy efforts. Naftalin and Brandl found "...the strategy has brought an undisputed measure of order to regional planning and has put in place a mechanism for dealing with complex regional problems" (pp. 63, 64). They cite a number of specific and positive outcomes of the work done in the 1970s.

In describing the relationship of the regional strategy to the inner city distressed areas (pp. 46, 47), they point out that the regional strategy does not separate out inner city distressed areas for special attention, but is intended to deal with all sections of the region. "In this relationship there is no point at which distress is identified as a clear and direct target for the attention of the strategy, although it remains a general and continuing regional concern."

To the author of this report, who was a Metropolitan Council professional planner and manager during that period, and very involved in developing the regional strategy, the Brandl and Naftalin judgment seems accurate, though generous. The purpose of most of the regional strategy was to achieve a balance between environmental concerns and regional facility funding and, at the same time, not reduce the amount of new development. The distress of inner cities was of some concern, but given much less attention than environmental and development issues.

Some policies that will help in the long run were developed: public investment priorities emphasizing developed areas over new development, an urban service area to stop unneeded extension of services, and policies and programs to place a limited amount of low income housing in suburbs. However, no policies were able, or expected, to stop the process of social and economic isolation of the inner cities that development processes and the housing market were bringing about.

City and Neighborhood Planning

The Minneapolis Plan for the 1980s considered population stability
as the vital city goal for that decade (Hearing Draft, Minneapolis
Planning Department, June, 1979, 1-13).
The goal is threefold:

> First, to help those low and moderate income per-
> sons who choose to or must live in the city to be
> economically self-sufficient—to obtain the essen-
> tials of living and to reduce or eliminate the barriers
> which prohibit participation in community life.

> Second, to retain those middle and upper income
> persons living in the city, now or in the future, who
> have the choice of leaving, particularly young
> families.

> Third, to attract present and potential middle and
> upper income persons to the city.

Neither the concern about inner city distress reflected throughout the Plan for the 1980s, nor the community-wide discussions of
the plan's preparation, nor the associated community-scale planning resulted in a strategy strong enough to resist the social changes
that took place in the 1980s. While the city's overall economy did
well, the inner city declined.

When the Plan for the 1980s was being prepared, a vigorous
debate took place among the Mayor's Office, the City Coordinator,
and the Planning Department about whether first priority in community development spending should be housing or economic
development. In retrospect, and notwithstanding whether anyone
won the debate, the 1980s resulted in more downtown private
economic investment than ever hoped for, strong increases in house
values and neighborhood strength in much of the city, and at least a
statistical stabilization in the overall quality of city housing. But,
the 1980s also saw a sharp decline in inner city social conditions, a
reasonable concern about a next tier of neighborhoods, and an
increasing tendency of residents to leave the city.

In 1988, the planning directors of the fifty largest U.S. cities
were surveyed by their professional organization to determine their
confidence about the future of their cities. They were asked how
optimistic or threatened they were about city economics, housing,
social, environmental, infrastructure and governmental structure.
From the twenty-seven respondents an interesting general picture
emerged.

The planning directors were quite optimistic about the overall
economic futures of their cities. The 1980s economic recovery,
downtown office construction, and some success in reestablishing
downtown retail facilities gave them some confidence.

Very few were optimistic about the future social well-being of their cities. The survey did not ask whether they felt that the city economic development efforts, or economic recovery in general, were connecting well with the needs of low income people and neighborhoods. But the disparity between their positive view about the general economic future and their skepticism about social well-being says they did not. It seems ironic that one can be separated from the other, i.e., that a place is economically strong but failing to meet the needs of its residents. What they obviously saw at city-scale was the national dichotomy of the 1980s, an apparently strong economy, accompanied by increasing crime, homelessness, infant mortality, drug use, and other measures of socioeconomic failure.

Perhaps the useful generalization is that in city after city an otherwise strong regional economy is failing to do something that a successful economy should be expected to do: distribute its strength into all neighborhoods and most households of the area. Similarly, metropolitan housing markets, while superficially doing well, were also failing to shelter people, with homeless people on the streets in close proximity to abandoned housing.

A specific concern is why otherwise successful downtown economic development efforts failed to have much direct effect upon inner city conditions. This is a matter of fit and scale. The proportion of jobs resulting from economic development that are likely to be filled by inner city low income people is so small that even a large number of such projects does not make a measurable impact on inner city conditions. This is not to say that the resulting employment and tax base increases do not help the long-term situation and provide some low income jobs, but downtown redevelopment is no solution to the inner city situation.

The survey, other discussion, and my visits to some of these cities in 1989 all indicate increasing attention to social, housing, and neighborhood issues and to finding deliberate ways to connect economic strength to economic need rather than trust some abstract concept such as "filtering down."

Most cities are revisiting neighborhood planning, at a fairly comprehensive level. Because the approaches are emerging independently and are tailored to fit the situations and politics of individual cities rather than the guidelines of any particularly federal program, a lot of experience will be gained with neighborhood-scale planning and programs during the next few years. At this point it is clear that the approaches are more comprehensive, people-oriented, and strategic than in the past. Communities are moving away from relying upon fixing houses or any other one program to remedy situations in troubled neighborhoods.

The Minneapolis twenty-year revitalization plan is as advanced as any city's plan, though some other places, i.e., Denver, may be moving more quickly with new, detailed and comprehensive neighborhood programs. Of course this is not all new. We have had the good fortune of strong neighborhood-based community development and housing activity for a long time, without which our present situation would be even more dire.

To this point we have been thinking about strategies by reviewing some of the national literature and some previous regional and city planning. But we cannot ignore the societal and economic trends that may change the inner city situation during the 1990s.

The Context in the 1990s

There is no reason to believe that the trends covered earlier will not continue, but it may be useful to look ahead a little and try to see what will be going on in the next decade that directly or indirectly may change inner city problems. The following are some trends and predictions for the next decade that will affect inner city possibilities and provide a context for a metropolitan and inner city strategy.

The 1990 census will verify the continuation and probably worsening of socioeconomic polarization and isolation at the national and metropolitan level. It is quite likely that society and cities will be economically more segregated than in 1980 and that racial separation will have changed little during the decade. Within cities, there will be a sharper economic differentiation among geographic areas than in 1980.

Increasing income and wage disparities have deepened problems during the 1980s. As our economy becomes more technical and more global, it seems likely that this trend will continue and will aggravate housing markets, social and economic segregation, and inner city problems unless there is considerably more intervention in income redistribution and/or the housing market.

The present attention and discussion of poverty, the underclass, and the culture of poverty by conservatives and liberals in government and academia may lead to some new ideas and programs. The discussion tends to divide into liberal and conservative camps. In general, liberals describe the causes as macroeconomic and structural while conservatives see such causes as family breakdown and individual character flaws. When each moves from description to prescription, they change lenses. Conservatives tend to advocate macroeconomic, structural, economic growth—the "rising tide lifts all boats" kinds of solutions. Liberals work on family and individual support systems.

In the 1990s, conservatives will continue to describe the problems in terms of people and family characteristics, but prescribe macroeconomics as the solution, i.e., capital gains and other regulatory adjustments to encourage the economy to produce jobs.

Liberals will continue to describe the problem in macroeconomic terms—lack of jobs and minimum wage—but prescribe social service solutions that address people and families. Both camps will agree that more reliance upon jobs and employment, rather than transfer payments, is the most politically viable and affordable way to bring most individuals out of poverty. Implementing this agreement will be difficult because it not only requires getting people ready to work, but also requires jobs that pay enough for single parents to earn a decent living in a time when income distribution policies and practices require even well-prepared families to have two jobs if they want a piece of the good life.

Perhaps enlightened self-interest will begin to replace tired ideology in some of these debates. The connections among such diverse issues as inner city poverty, international competition, the quality and the quantity of the labor force, and the demographics of the Social Security system, may become better understood and help enlighten self-interest. Consider the future: most retirees are white, most new workers are not white; by about 2010 only three workers will be available to finance each Social Security retiree, compared to fourteen today. The weak political leadership of the 1980s and 1990s failed to advance fund the Social Security system. Thus, today's inner city conditions and tomorrow's racially diverse labor force are intimately tied to the future strength of the Social Security system—the quality of retirement for today's workers.

Perhaps we will also see that the more people we must, or choose to, put in prison today, the more former prison inmates will concentrate in inner cities tomorrow. We need to either break out of imprisonment as a solution to social problems, or see to it that prisons become a training ground for competence and success in other than illicit activity. Or plan to hire more and tougher police officers and build more large prisons. Today's choices breed tomorrow's problems.

Because social and economic problems are at the heart of inner city situations, breaking people out of this cycle is central to a long-term inner city strategy. Increased attention to education and the well-being of children in the next decade should be factored into a metropolitan inner city strategy.

The current level of concern about drugs will go somewhere in the next decade. The immediate, highly visible impact of drugs on inner city conditions may be reduced, but the use of drugs and the resulting impact upon education, health and employment in the inner city will not be eliminated. If the recent emphasis results in a long-term commitment to adequate drug prevention and rehabilitation programs, along with drug law enforcement, inner city conditions will improve.

There will, in the 1990s, be a gradual and modest return of the
federal government to focus on social and inner city issues, probably not as urban policy per se, but as national human service and
people programs.

Two frequently cited forecasts for the 1990s are labor shortages and a reduction in demand for housing, both driven by the
demographic forecast of fewer young adults of working and home-
buying ages. The former could decrease inner city joblessness. The
latter could reduce relative prices of lower-priced housing, making
it more available to the lower and moderate income households
who may have more income due to less joblessness. This situation
would increase abandonment of the lowest quality housing stock,
i.e., the inner city. However, if the shift is only from joblessness to
working poor, a population frozen in low-paying service jobs, the
connection to the housing market is unclear.

The 1990s will bring a much reduced demographic demand for
added housing units, which will either lead to much less new construction or greatly increased inner city abandonment, as better
housing choices open up in a buyer's market. The forecast is for a
sharp reduction in the rate of growth of the total housing stock.
However, the forecast is not for a negative demand or a reduction in
the total number of units needed. This need not result in a glut of
housing or excessive abandonment and under-investment in the
existing stock.

Abandonment of existing housing will also be a function of the
rate of new construction. By whatever amount construction of new
units exceeds the formation of new households, existing units,
mostly the lowest quality ones, will be abandoned, demolished or
replaced. There will be a marketing tug of war between the efforts
of the housing industry to keep selling and building many units, and
the efforts of cities to prevent further weakening of the market for
existing housing, and abandonment of inner city neighborhoods.

The reduced demand for new housing will lead to a new
economically driven social consciousness in the housing industry,
which will begin advocating new government programs. Some of
these programs will sound a lot like urban renewal. They will
initially overemphasize new construction; they will not reflect very
well the needs of cities and mid-sized metropolitan areas.

It will be important that the metropolitan and city policy
makers enter actively into these housing discussions. The interests
of the housing industry consortium of builders, bankers and bureaucrats will not be identical to those of the cities, and those who need
housing.

The same drop in the population of young adults that is
expected to slow housing demand should also mean reduced growth
of the labor supply, which may lead to labor shortages, and higher

employment rates. Most new jobs will continue to be in the suburbs. At some point this labor shortage will be interrupted or ended by a recession.

Current environmental predictions of serious ozone depletion and temperature warming due to the greenhouse effect will become generally accepted as accurate, stimulating rigorous new environmental standards and serious debate about the appropriateness, necessity, and means of economic growth and transportation regulation. This will divert attention from social issues.

Even the automobile manufacturers will ask for new federal emissions and gasoline consumption regulations to override a wave of diverse legislation by states and cities, which will continue to be far ahead of the federal government in understanding environmental issues. New national transportation legislation which does not deal with environmental reality will be adopted in the early 1990s. It will be followed, later in the 1990s, by crisis legislation.

Construction of new space for office, residential, retail and perhaps industrial uses will be reduced in the 1990s. Demand for built space, the final product of redevelopment, will be weak, making redevelopment a difficult means to city revitalization. The housing market will be saturated due to demographic changes; office space will be at a saturation point due to excess construction in the 1980s and a slowing of the shift to a service-oriented, office-based economy. Retail markets will be saturated and in chaos due to excessive construction in the 1980s and early 1990s.

Industrial demand and resulting space and employment needs are not so clear. A highly competitive, increasingly international economy in which many markets are saturated will make finding new markets a high priority. Markets may be more difficult to find than new products, depending upon the growth of purchasing power in developing and eastern European countries. Corporations and investment will be mobile, seeking not only markets, but (to avoid environmental and social brinksmanship) production and administrative centers that appear to have their societal and environmental act together.

Obviously, these predictions are interdependent. If markets are easily found, then the labor shortage will be greater and inflation may be the issue. If environmental problems are real and severe, production and labor surplus will be more of an issue, markets and labor supply less. The nineties will be an interesting decade, with new barriers but also opportunities to do something about inner city decline.

Toward a Strategy

Given this context, what are some obvious city and metropolitan strategies to deal with inner city problems?

The housing industry should turn its attention to low and moderate income housing with better proximity to jobs. We should try to localize housing abandonment into as few areas as possible. Lots of "people" programs may be needed to deal with the difficult people and neighborhood situations left behind in partially abandoned neighborhoods. We probably should not get into major clearance and renewal projects in any given area until the "people" issues are being better dealt with, probably not in the 1990s.

The size of the poverty situation with which the metropolitan area and the inner city must cope will be largely determined by national and state actions. If poverty increases, inner city problems will increase. Relative success within this imperative requires an economic, housing and transportation strategy that works at the household, neighborhood and metropolitan levels. Metropolitan planning as we know it now deals mostly with engineering issues. When it develops an explicit metropolitan-scale human development and inner city strategy, it will move into genuine urban planning. This does not mean that metropolitan agencies should begin to do neighborhood planning; it means they should devise and put in place strategies to change the regional forces that create inner city situations that help cities and neighborhood activists succeed.

The long-term solution and highest priority of a strategy must address human development and poverty. It must deal with weak families, education and income in ways such as those recommended by Sawhill and discussed in the next chapter.

A theme that runs through all thinking and writing about social and inner city strategies is joblessness and under-employment as cause and effect of family breakdown. Unprepared job seekers, the nature and location of new jobs, and lack of job growth are all part of the puzzle. Lack of jobs in certain areas is a problem the Twin Cities share with the rest of Minnesota. It should be addressed by a cooperative state, metropolitan and local economic development program that pays close attention to type, location and access to new jobs. Employment and investment in economically troubled parts of outstate Minnesota and the inner city should take priority in this cooperative program. The otherwise strong metropolitan economy should be viewed as a magnet to attract growth in the national and international economy, then spin off to the inner cities and outstate Minnesota.

We should take the fullest possible advantage of the predicted 1990s labor shortage, to the extent that it is real and continues. The goal should be to bring people into employment and do everything possible to see that they don't just fall out of employment again when the shortage is past. We should make training beyond rudimentary skills a part of the employment situation, and also use the labor shortage as leverage to get people "mainstreamed" into housing, equities, careers, sound neighborhoods, education, their children's education, health insurance, retirement plans, and protection from future economic downturn.

A successful strategy must deal explicitly with how and where low income housing will be provided. The national and metropolitan housing de facto policy is that most low income housing will be provided by devaluation of inner city neighborhoods. Without financial support to adequately house all low income households in the cities and/or the suburbs, additional city neighborhoods will decline. Under present constraints, successful efforts to revitalize, in a market sense, city neighborhoods will result in decline somewhere else, or put people in the street or under bridges. Housing strategies that intend to both revitalize neighborhoods and provide adequate low income shelter without explicitly dealing with the conflicts between the two goals are, under present parameters, naive and unachievable. This question must be explicitly resolved for a successful inner city strategy.

Strategy Summary

The premise here is that an effective strategy must apply to elements throughout the inner city system (Figure 6). Not enough can be done with any one element to achieve satisfactory results. It should be designed to be synergistic. Work on one aspect will achieve results in others, and work on all fronts will yield cumulative results.

The strategy should be coordinated, supportive and interdependent, but not dependent. It is naive to expect an open democratic process to endorse, fund and implement a comprehensive system simultaneously. The effort should be to intervene in the inner city decline process by eliminating or reducing a cause or by disconnecting a cause-and-effect relationship. If only limited segments or scale are put in place, the problems will not be solved, but some improvement could result from the effort.

Figure 6. Strategies to Reverse Path of Decline in Inner Cities

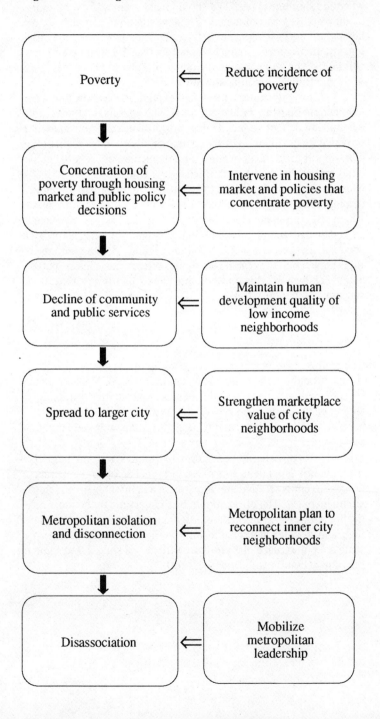

Those impatient with grand strategies and big solutions might find it more comfortable to view this as the outline of a work program, budget book and intergovernmental relations and lobbying agenda for a city that intends to significantly improve inner city problems and curtail their spread to more of the city.

Because problems and solutions are interconnected, sometimes circular, there are choices about where to begin. City- and metropolitan-scale work on inner city conditions best begins with poverty reduction. One could begin close to the root causes of poverty (the following chapter discusses what those are). However, at the detail presented here, "poverty" seems the beginning of both problems and solutions.

First, if an accurate full-scale poverty program could be put into effect that eliminated poverty, the rest of this approach would seem unnecessary. The rest of the work could concentrate on physical conditions and marketing. In fact, in the absence of poverty and racism, the inner city would probably do quite nicely in the marketplace, given its proximity, centrality, urbanity and housing uniqueness.

Elimination of poverty would reduce negative racial attitudes and some of their power to damage lives. In a market in which all households had substantial legal and economic choice in housing location, whether racial separation patterns would remain is beyond this study. It is the premise here that reducing racism will reduce poverty, that reducing poverty will reduce racism, and that reducing either or both is necessary for lasting improvement in inner city conditions. If poverty increases, inner city conditions will deepen and spread to more of the city and metropolitan area, notwithstanding other efforts. More emphasis is given to the poverty side of the discussion in Chapter Four. More study is needed on racial issues and the author is continuing to research and prepare future writing on this subject.

Second, while we do know a lot about how to eliminate poverty, not enough will be done externally. Therefore, an inner city strategy must reduce the housing market concentration of poverty in the inner city. It must prevent service overburden as a further cause of poverty; prevent the spread of inner city conditions throughout the central city; maintain some demographic, resource, economic and cultural balance; and prevent large poverty concentrations that will become more spatially, economically and culturally isolated from metropolitan opportunity. Chapter Five covers metropolitan housing policy and choice in housing location programs designed to reduce inner city poverty.

Third, in the absence of any immediate success in poverty reduction, there will be a clear responsibility for central city governance. This is to prevent low income and poverty residential areas

from becoming breeding grounds for further poverty. The mission
could be stated as maintaining high standards of human development in poverty areas. This is largely a municipal and community
function, deserving of resource assistance from other levels of
government.

Maintaining human development characteristics is largely a
municipal and community function; and is as much about traditional public safety, public health, education and general neighborhood services as about housing, social services and economic
development programs. This is covered in Chapter Six.

Fourth, because it is vital to the interests of all income groups
that the entire central city not be overtaken by inner city conditions,
the strength in the private metropolitan housing market of most
central city neighborhoods must be preserved. Poverty, concentration reduction, and maintaining human development conditions in
low income areas will help preserve market strength and enhance
the efforts of those working at the neighborhood level. However,
none of this will proceed far or fast enough to eliminate the need
for work on neighborhood stabilization. Chapter Seven further
elaborates the importance and means of neighborhood stabilization.
It also stresses that neighborhood revitalization and low income
shelter provision are two different things, and require careful policy
distinction.

Fifth, metropolitan-scale development patterns and practices,
transportation networks, and employment patterns are catalysts of
inner city poverty concentration and the isolation that perpetuates
it. This needs to be addressed with metropolitan planning that emphasizes reconnection—breaking down the isolation of the inner
city neighborhood and households. This means both reconnection
in a physical sense and more subtle attention to social, cultural and
economic patterns. It directly concerns development planning, the
fundamental arena of metropolitan planning agencies. The need for
a new vision, and the ends and means of metropolitan development,
are discussed in Chapter Eight.

Sixth, a city, metropolitan and state leadership coalition with a
sense of shared responsibility for inner city conditions, and a
unified commitment to a long-term strategy and resources for solution are needed. This involves education and persuasion that this is
not just a city problem; agreement upon a strategy; assignment and
acceptance of responsibility for implementation by all levels; and
partnerships among households, neighborhoods, cities, metropolitan and state agencies to make decisions and get things done. This
and questions of resources and distribution are covered in Chapter
Nine.

In summary, the six agenda items needed to address inner city conditions are there:

- Working to reduce the incidence of poverty.
- Intervening in the housing market concentration of poverty in the inner city.
- Maintaining, in spite of difficult circumstances, the human development quality of low income neighborhoods.
- Strengthening the marketplace value of city neighborhoods in the metropolitan housing market.
- Developing a metropolitan plan to reconnect rather than further disconnect and isolate the inner city from metropolitan opportunity.
- Mobilizing metropolitan leadership to share in the responsibility and solutions to inner city and poverty issues.

A strategy is more than a list of things to do. It is about what needs to be done first, or even doing several mutually supportive things at once rather than the panacea-of-the-year approach. It requires responses that are at the scale of the problem and continue long enough to make a difference. We must make sure, for example, that the housing programs and poverty programs are mutually supportive and that both are supported rather than negated by transportation policy. Strategy demands setting up new and eliminating old organizations to focus on the desired end rather than forcing a definition of desired end that fits the existing organization. Strategy is complex and, in the real political and bureaucratic world, action can, at best, only roughly approach being "strategic" in the way discussed here.

A lot of existing programs may fit into this six-point strategy. Among them are redrawn or dissolved school district boundaries; metropolitan school integration; expanding the regional park system to a green belt, along with statewide development to manage urban sprawl; a metropolitan housing utility; transportation ideas; welfare reform; and new interest in federal housing legislation.

Effective strategy elements should pass these tests:

- They must serve to integrate and reconnect isolated households and neighborhoods; those plans that further isolate should be rejected, no matter how tempting in the short run.
- Acceptance or rejection of ideas should be on the basis of effect upon the situation rather than existing institutions. For example, school change, and most other change, should be based almost entirely upon whether it is good for children and very little on preservation of existing arrangements.

- Elements should not neutralize one another, but could compete with one another for a piece of the solution and, at best, would leverage one another for some synergistic effect.
- A successful strategy must operate at the scale of the problem. Many attempts are minuscule compared to the need, but put in place someone's favorite and perhaps very good idea and make us feel like the problem is solved.

It is clear that no one plan will solve the metropolitan inner city situation. No city or metropolitan area has made significant progress with just one program. To be successful we must learn to do several things at once. In housing, the livability of inner city neighborhoods must be addressed while offering more suburban choices for low income households. Poverty, shelter, housing markets, transportation, economic development, human services and the environment must be addressed together in cooperative and mutually supportive ways.

Chapter Four

Proposals for a Metropolitan-Scale Poverty Agenda

> Thus, the paradox: millions of jobs might be going
> begging, but huge numbers of Americans remained
> either unemployed or unemployable. Circum-
> stances like this resulted in the destitution and
> homelessness that perturbed cities and suburbs
> everywhere as economic polarization intensified.
>
> Kevin Philips, 1990, p. 20.

The conclusion that reducing poverty must be the first element in a
strategy to improve inner city conditions is obvious, but uncomfortable. Such a conclusion means that analysis and action must move
from the comfort of discussing house and pavement conditions to
much more intangible and intransigent people and social issues. It
means moving into the morass of intergovernmental relations. For
the author of this report, with a background more in the physical
and administrative side of city planning than in the sociological, it
means an old dog must try to learn new tricks.

Notwithstanding this discomfort, it is clear that a city that
wants to improve its future must have a very active poverty agenda
working at the federal, state, metropolitan and city level and that its
housing and other agendas must be consistent with its poverty
agenda. This is a necessary condition of making progress on inner
city conditions and reducing their spread.

The purpose of this chapter is to present some thinking about
approaches. It is not put forth as the complete, final or only way,
but to show that poverty issues can be part of an inner city improvement strategy and that there are ways to proceed. If poverty
increases throughout society, more poverty shelter will be needed
in the metropolitan area and most of that need will be met by
devaluing more central city neighborhoods. This is not the only con-
sequence of a national failure to deal with poverty, but it is one that
greatly affects the city.

Part of the poverty agenda the city must accomplish itself. This has to do with maintaining the livability and human development characteristics of low income neighborhoods so that these neighborhoods do not become further causes of poverty. This mostly concerns results-oriented delivery of traditional city services and community building. This is discussed in Chapter Six.

Anthony Downs, writing in 1985, believed that prior to the 1980s our society had reached a consensus on a "send money" approach to racial and poverty issues. In the 1980s we reverted to acceptance of them as inevitable.

Downs recalls that the Kerner Commission on Civil Disorder in 1968 discussed three possible strategies for responding to inner city and racial problems: one of continuing "present policies" of segregation and poverty; another a "ghetto enrichment" strategy of continuing segregation combined with federal, city and individual financial assistance; and a third strategy of deliberate integration combined with ghetto enrichment. While the Kerner Commission rejected the first two and unanimously recommended the third, Downs points out that the country actually followed, through the 1970s, a policy of "mild ghetto enrichment and continued segregation." In the 1980s we reverted to the 1968 "present policy" of both poverty and segregation that the Kerner Commission had rejected as the "worst possible alternative for America" (Anthony Downs, "The Future of Industrial Cities," in *The New Urban Reality*, The Brookings Institute, 1985, 288).

Downs' conclusion about the 1980s fits the worsening of inner city conditions that took place and can be observed in most central cities. It fits the data and logic presented in Chapter Two, which show that economic and political changes in the 1980s had a concentrated, devastating impact upon inner city areas weakened by decades of demographic, social and economic metropolitan development trends.

My views on poverty have been enhanced by observing other cities and examining some of the extensive research and writing being done throughout the country. The following pages summarize some of the best of that research, primarily to present some strategic ideas.

Mark Allen Hughes, in his work for the National League of Cities, recommends a six-point "mobility strategy" as the appropriate response to poverty problems. "The point of this strategy is to reconnect the ghetto to opportunity. That connection has been disrupted by metropolitan decentralization and other factors. The components of the mobility strategy are designed to restore that connection by exploiting the very incentives created by decentralization itself" (*Poverty in Cities*, National League of Cities, Washington, D.C., 1989, 18).

Hughes rejects strategies that hope to solve the problems caused by metropolitan decentralization through either dispersal of low income housing or development to recentralize regional employment. He believes that housing dispersal strategies ignore the sociology of the problem and job recentralization strategies ignore the economics of the problem. The proposal suggested later in this report includes both dispersal and development, but does not rely either on moving jobs or low income housing as the single solution.

The six-point mobility strategy Hughes recommends consists of job training, regional job information systems, restructuring transportation for outbound work trips, day care while training, job seeking and working, increased earned income credits for low income employee employers, and community policing (pp. 17, 18).

While working primarily in areas more impacted than the Twin Cities, and advising that his recommendations be adapted as needed, he urges approaches that work with rather than try to change economic trends. He particularly recommends the predicted labor shortage of the 1990s as an opportunity to be exploited.

Isabel Sawhill of the Urban Institute has researched and written extensively about national social, political, and economic issues. Sawhill notes that attention to a number of social and poverty problems is insufficient. "Although all these groups need help, it will be argued here that the nation's top priority should be to stem the growth of chronic poverty and the underclass" ("Poverty and the Underclass," in *Challenge to Leadership*, The Urban Institute, Washington, D.C., 1988, Isabel Sawhill, ed., 231).

Sawhill's research lead her to conclude about poverty from 1967 to 1985:

1. The poverty rate is about the same at the end as at the beginning of the period.

2. Two factors were clearly pushing up the poverty rate: demographics and the poor performance of the economy.

3. At the same time, anti-poverty policies were working to reduce the poverty rate. In the absence of increased spending, an additional 5 million to 12 million would now be poor, and many of those who remain poor would be far worse off (p. 220).

Sawhill believes the "root causes" of persistent poverty are "weak families, substantial joblessness, and poor education" (p. 247) and that a self-sufficiency strategy for the underclass "is probably best advanced through policies that strengthen parents' responsibility for their children, encourage work, and improve education" (p. 231).

Sawhill recommends parental responsibility programs to prevent early childbearing, collect child support, and encourage welfare mothers to work. She advocates work encouragement programs related to full employment and training, increasing the rewards for working, and expansion of proven education programs like Headstart, compensatory education and Jobs Corps.

William Julius Wilson is a leading thinker and writer about national social and racial issues. His book, *The Truly Disadvantaged*, provides insight into how this country got into its present social crisis and what approaches could help solve it. His points are so well-analyzed and carefully made that only reading his entire book does justice to his work. However, the following quotation makes some of his major points about the national situation; this description at least partially fits the Twin Cities.

> If I had to use one term to capture the differences in the experiences of low-income families who live in inner-city areas from the experiences of those who live in other areas in the central city today, that term would be concentration effects. The social transformation of the inner city has resulted in a disproportionate concentration of the most disadvantaged segments of the urban black population, creating a social milieu significantly different from the environment that existed in these communities several decades ago (p. 58).

> The key theoretical concept is not culture of poverty, but social isolation (p. 60).

In a recent address, Wilson cited research and surveys he has conducted in inner city Chicago neighborhoods since his book was published. From that recent research he concludes that inner city black people overwhelmingly share values about work that are essentially the same as mainstream America's; that the problem is not one of people not believing in work as the way out of poverty ("Social Isolation: A New Look at the Problems of Race and Poverty in the Inner City Ghetto," May 30, 1990, University of Wisconsin, Madison).

Wilson does put joblessness at the root of the problem. The structural shifts away from manufacturing, and the shift of remaining manufacturing jobs to the suburbs, away from lower income residential areas, are seen as major causes of this joblessness. Wilson is clear that it is not a "culture of poverty" problem, that it isn't that people don't want jobs, but a situation of jobs moving away geographically and in skill requirements. He presents convincing evidence that this joblessness, particularly among black males, is an underlying cause of social breakdown. He rejects the idea that the welfare system is the cause of the problem. "We conclude, therefore, that the problem of joblessness should be a top-priority item in any public policy discussion focusing on enhancing the status of families" (p. 105).

Wilson is speaking at the national scale, but his emphasis on joblessness as a cause of the problem, and employment opportunity as a key part of the solution, should be considered basic to economic development strategies at any level.

> I have in mind a general economic policy that would involve long-term planning to promote both economic growth and sustained full employment, not only in higher-income areas, but in areas where the poor are concentrated as well. Such a policy would be designed to promote wage and price stability, favorable employment conditions, and the development and integration of manpower training with educational programs. As I see it, the questions usually ignored when ad hoc strategies to promote employment are discussed and proposed should be systematically addressed. These questions include the relative impact of proposed strategies on labor markets in different areas of the country: the type, variety, and volume of jobs to be generated; the extent to which residents in low-income neighborhoods will have access to these jobs; the quality of these jobs in terms of stability and pay; the extent to which proposed strategies to enhance the employment opportunities of both new entrants into the labor market and the currently employed; and whether the benefits from economic development provide reasonable returns on public investment (p. 121).

Wilson makes it clear that he supports a broad economic strategy because he believes it will benefit those most needy, while being politically more realistic than race- or poverty-specific programs.

John Kasarda has done long-term analysis of economic and job shifts in urban areas and also puts a good deal of emphasis on joblessness as a major component of inner city problems. He describes the general national situation in terms of functional changes in the economy; loss of some kinds of central city jobs, particularly manufacturing; increasing educational requirements of those jobs; and confinement of minorities in inner city areas as jobs decentralize. "Serious problems of racial discrimination, inadequate transportation, and insufficient low income housing in areas of employment growth further obstruct mobility and job acquisition"

(Kasarda, "Urban Change and Minority Opportunities," in *The New Urban Reality*, The Brooking Institution, 1985, Paul E. Peterson, ed., 60).

Kasarda calls for a change in policy emphasis:

> Politically popular (but ineffective) jobs-to-people programs and essential urban welfare programs must be better balanced with serious efforts to upgrade the education and skills of disadvantaged city residents and with people-to-jobs strategies that would facilitate the migration of the structurally unemployed to places where job opportunities appropriate to their skills are still expanding (p. 66).

> To increase the mobility of the urban disadvantaged, revised policies should be considered that would partially underwrite their more distant job searches and relocation expenses. Additional policies must be aimed at further reducing housing and employment discrimination and other institutional impediments to the mobility of minorities who wish to leave distressed urban areas. Finally, existing public assistance programs should be reviewed to ensure that they are not inadvertently attracting or bonding large numbers of disadvantaged persons to inner city areas that offer limited opportunities for employment (p. 66).

Kasarda is clearly more persuaded than Hughes of the necessity and possibility of strategies involving low income housing location. However, he does not offer it as the single solution. In general, he characterizes his approach as one that jointly addresses issues of race, space, and education.

Gary Orfield has analyzed the Chicago inner city situation. Orfield believes that both school and housing integration need to be pursued and notes the decades-long slide into the present Chicago situation (Gary Orfield, "Ghettoization and its Alternatives," in *The New Urban Reality*, 1985).

> Chicago is not helpless in the face of ghettoization. City officials contributed powerfully to the creation and maintenance of the process, but they have never attempted to mobilize resources against it. They have instead engaged in denial of the problem or quixotic attacks on its symptoms. Some communities in the Chicago area, however, have achieved a good deal of success with virtually no help from the higher levels of government and sometimes despite their policies. Much could be

done to move toward the only alternative the city
has to the continuation of the destructive process of
the last seventy years, residential and school integration. It would not be a panacea, but it is a
necessary part of any strategy for reviving the city
and avoiding needless loss of additional resources.
A fully developed strategy would, of course,
include employment and economic development,
compensatory education, adult education, and other
social and economic programs addressing the
accumulated inequalities in minority communities.
Though an integration policy would serve the end
of racial justice, it need not be undertaken for that
reason. In a society with Chicago's racial composi-
tion and social and economic patterns, it is a matter
of simple self interest (p. 193).

Orfield further urges "as many well integrated schools as possible
within the city, while pushing in every possible way for involvement of the suburbs in the school integration process" (p. 192).

As an advocate also of dispersed housing choices, Orfield
describes the experience of the Chicago Housing Authority in
placing families in private housing in outer suburbs. "By 1984, however, the number of families placed in this program had passed
2,000. The demand for available spaces each year has been over-
whelming. When families who had moved to the suburbs were
interviewed, four-fifths were satisfied with their new homes and
neighborhoods and nine-tenths with their local schools and
teachers. Early participants in the program reported little white
hostility in their new neighborhoods. The families' employment
had increased, and only 2 percent said they were interested in
returning to the city" (p. 191). The housing dispersal program discussed above by Orfield has also been analyzed by James E.
Rosenbaum and Susan J. Popkin at Northwestern University.

The "Gautreaux Program" grew out of a 1976 Supreme Court
decision that set out a metropolitan-wide response to discrimination
in Chicago's public housing. The program has now placed about
3,500 public housing families in suburban locations. The research
compares the experiences of those in the suburban locations to
those families that remained in the city. In 1982, a study of how
children fared in the suburbs found "the outcomes for the suburban
movers were generally very positive, although they had to contend
with more demanding schools, a dramatically different environment, and some racism from teachers and peers" (James E.
Rosenbaum and Susan E. Popkin, *The Gautreaux Program: An Experiment in Racial and Economic Integration, The Center Report,*
Center for Urban Affairs and Policy Research, Northwestern

University, Vol. 2, No. 1, Spring, 1990). That study of the children is being continued as the first group approaches age twenty.

The current study compared the experience of mothers moving into the suburbs with public housing mothers who moved into improved central city housing. Suburban movers were found to be as integrated into their community as the city group, despite some initial racial problems. While the program had no employment component, the suburban movers were more likely to be employed. Those employed before the move were more likely than those who stayed in the city to have found new employment; those unemployed before the move were more likely to have found employment. The authors believe the study supports the idea that lack of access to jobs is part of the urban poverty problem. Rosenbaum found that families continued to prefer the suburban locations, that school achievement was better for these children than those remaining in inner city housing, and that more adults had found employment.

In general, national writers on these issues range from those who tend to see the problems as weaknesses in people and the welfare system, i.e., the culture of poverty and unwillingness to work, to the more liberal writers who tend to see the problems as system failures, i.e., the failure of the economy to provide available and accessible jobs.

Perhaps the most persuaded writer of the conservative viewpoint is Charles Murray (*Losing Ground: American Social Policy 1950-1980*, New York, Basic Books, 1984). His premise is that increased poverty results from too much rather than too little public effort. His analysis is intended to show that increases in public poverty-related expenditures are followed by an increase in the problem. His further premise is the classic argument that welfare relieves individuals of the consequences of irresponsible actions. They won't learn to act responsibly unless we get rid of welfare systems. Just how children, the handicapped, the elderly, and those heretofore unprepared for work by the educational system are to handle their responsibilities is not clear.

It is sometimes possible to solve today's problems tomorrow, or prevent tomorrow's problems by today's actions, but it is not possible to solve today's problems yesterday. Lamenting family breakdown and the welfare system as the cause of today's unprepared, troubled or troublesome adults may help in the future, but will not provide the programs needed to deal with problems already here.

If there is a societal consensus about poverty reduction it is that it will come through employment rather than transfer payments. This means a metropolitan strategy must include jobs, people prepared for those jobs, and jobs or job-related income supplements sufficient to bring the typical single-parent family out of poverty. This will be difficult in an economy in which even well-prepared families typically need two wage earners.

These writers are at least partially describing and prescribing for the national societal situation, while the purpose here is a metropolitan approach. However, their ideas have application at the metropolitan and city scale. Poverty must become a basic part of the metropolitan-scale planning and legislative agenda. Its concentration in the inner city is a metropolitan phenomenon. Almost all of the major metropolitan-scale planning items are related to poverty issues. That includes at least transportation, housing, development patterns, job distribution, public services of all kinds, racial and economic integration, and education. Those who don't see a new agenda of critical metropolitan planning issues apparently don't want serious metropolitan involvement in these most important urban problems of poverty and inner city conditions.

Rather than focus on a single approach, a panacea-of-the-year, it is essential to decide if we want quick results or a fundamental correction. We probably need programs designed for immediate, though sometimes symptomatic, results; programs for intermediate-term, more fundamental results; and programs designed for long-term, fundamental change. This is illustrated in Figure 7 and described below.

We can get the fastest results from programs oriented toward weak and single-parent families. Improving the parenting skills, shelter opportunities and stability, nutrition, day care, health care, and income in these situations should show immediate results in the well-being of adults, particularly women, and both immediate and long-term improvement in the life chances of children.

We need and should expect longer-term results from programs that include an emphasis on employment, particularly reducing adult male joblessness. This thinking is connected to Julius Wilson's research that assigns adult male joblessness a major causal role in single-parent, frequently weak families.

Figure 7. Changing Program Emphasis in Results-Oriented Poverty Strategies

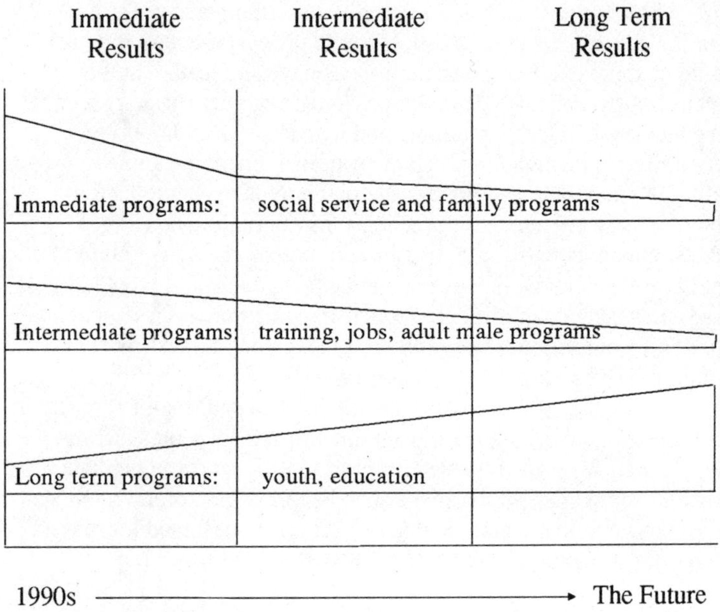

Immediate Results	Intermediate Results	Long Term Results

Immediate programs:	social service and family programs
Intermediate programs:	training, jobs, adult male programs
Long term programs:	youth, education

1990s ⟶ The Future

The importance of single-parent families to the poverty issue can be revealed by simple arithmetic. If all else were equal and if all adults' incomes were equal, single-parent households would immediately have one-half the average income of two-working-parent households. All else isn't equal. The average income per adult, particularly among women who head most single-parent families, is less; the costs of parenting are higher; and poverty is inevitably much more prevalent among single parents. Since 1959 the percentage of female-headed households in poverty has dropped only from 42 percent to 34 percent, and remained unchanged since 1966. Male-headed family poverty rates have dropped by over half, from 15.8 percent to 7.0 percent ("The Feminization of Poverty," Steven Pressman, *Challenge Magazine*, April 1988, 57).

The conservative view of the importance of this is expressed by Chester E. Finn, Jr. in his paper and address to the Center for the American Experiment ("Ten Tentative Truths," April and June, 1990, 4).

> With rare exceptions, two-parent families are good
> for children, one-parent families are bad, zero-

parent families are horrible. This is not something to be ashamed of. It is the product of the species' experience in billions of instances spanning the millennia. Nor is it the only wisdom we've acquired. We know, too, that, with rare exceptions, a couple that has children must remain a couple if the children are to be well-served. We know that people who are not married—or joined in some other stable fashion—should not have children.

Now for some verbal alchemy. Chester E. Finn, as a conservative thinker about education and social issues, is certain that single-parent families are very bad for children. Julius Wilson, a more liberal thinker about race and poverty, is convinced and convincing that adult male joblessness leading to a shortage of marriageable adult males is a major cause of the single-parent situation among low income blacks. If we connect these two views, a connection to which each author might object, it becomes evident that successful intervention in the poverty cycle must address joblessness among adult males, particularly adult black males, in order to get at the problems of children.

However, unless there are jobs available, accessible, and remunerative enough to make working worthwhile, training will not accomplish the purpose. Wilson's ideas about full employment economies and economic growth that produce the kind and location of jobs needed, and Kasarda's ideas about transportation and housing, must also be considered.

Programs that will make a permanent difference are those that get people and neighborhoods reconnected to the larger society, economy and opportunity. Those that don't reconnect may look like solutions, but fixing houses, reforming welfare, or arresting people are band-aids on serious wounds. The problems will simply reoccur later, in the same place or somewhere else.

New attention to these problems, combined with predicted demographic trends in housing and job markets, should improve inner city conditions during the next decade. However, these changes will not solve the problems—though attention to the problem may diminish. Unless we are also successful in reconnecting inner city people and neighborhoods with the larger society and economy and in changing the forces that continuously bring about social and economic separation, the basic conditions will remain— destroying life chances and the core of the city; awaiting the next cycle of downturn in the economy, changes in human service funding, or further economic restructuring to re-emerge as visible and popular crises.

It is a mistake to view the demographic reduction in new job seekers and the oft-predicted labor shortages expected in the 1990s as the solution to poverty and inner city problems. They may represent a wave of opportunity that proactive public action can exploit for permanent improvements. But if merely observed and not acted upon, the demographic changes will lead to increased abandonment of housing scattered throughout much of the inner city, damaging neighborhoods and lives. It could also lead to many people trained to be minimum-wage workers, unprepared either for subsequent economic downturn or active citizenship. Expectations should be higher. Capitalism and democracy need not only workers, but entrepreneurs, innovators, business owners, and participating citizens.

Taking advantage of the demographic trends of the 1990s will require proactive metropolitan strategies designed to connect as many households as possible, not only to training, but to education; not only to jobs, but to trades, professions, careers, benefits and business ownership; not only to shelter, but to homes, equity and neighborhoods.

Perhaps most difficult is not just connecting people to income, but to an accurate belief among those susceptible to poverty that there is a relationship between education, effort, useful work and success. The lessons of the 1980s, from Wall Street to "crack alley," from Pennsylvania Avenue to Madison Avenue, have been that hype, consumerism, dope dealing and other fast-buck deals— growth by parasitism—are more effective than innovation, entrepreneurism, productive economy building work and investment. That 1980s indoctrination will take some overcoming. But successful intervention in the poverty cycle depends on changes in the distribution of hope, incentive, work, pay scales, income and wealth. If, in fact, there is low probability that education and work will appreciably improve one's situation, people will remain with or move into such proven systems as public assistance, crime, or high finance rather than risk change. On the other hand, Julius Wilson's recent research in Chicago shows that residents of even the most difficult inner city areas overwhelmingly share prevailing middle class values about work, jobs, and income.

Conservatives should continue to insist that a poverty strategy emphasize individual responsibility and that there be negative consequences for irresponsible behavior in all social, income, and economic sectors. Liberals should once again insist on the economic structural changes needed to ensure that those who do live, learn, and work responsibly receive their fair share; that there be positive consequences for responsible behavior in all social, income, and economic sectors. At the risk of disguising rhetoric as thought, I would suggest that this could be the basis for an employment and income strategy that could begin to make a difference within a relatively short time.

Many of the key elements needed for long-term, fundamental success in "breaking the cycle of poverty" are already being discussed or put in place: youth programs, educational improvement, health care, and the amount of attention finally being given to underparented children in difficult neighborhoods.

A key to successful long-term results from education is to recognize that general education reform may not get at the particular needs of inner city children. For example, students choosing schools and programs may generally be good reform, but does not solve the much more difficult and important problem of teachers trying to teach large classrooms of unprepared, underparented, and perhaps undernourished and undersheltered children.

Most educational reform discussion is about middle-class solutions to middle-class problems and not about the most severe failings of the education system. The solutions to these problems have to do with preschool preparation of all underparented children; manageable class sizes, much smaller than the middle-class norm; and guarantees that anyone completing high school with enough knowledge to be admitted to additional education will have the financial support to get that higher education.

A city that offered universal preschool opportunity; much smaller class sizes; and guaranteed, visible, uncomplicated, universal financial access to higher education for its prepared high school graduates would not only have a much improved education system, it would have created more market strength for its housing and neighborhoods than any housing program could do.

There are enough problems to go around and a metropolitan poverty approach might want to test a range of humane ideas from both the conservative and liberal sides of the agenda, provided that they do not neutralize or conflict with one another. No single panacea, i.e., welfare reform or dispersed low income housing or job training, will, by itself, solve the long-term situations.

I am by no means an expert on the complex underlying causes of poverty. However, it is clear from what is going on in Minnesota and around the country that we know a lot about solutions. A great deal more is being learned in research and demonstrations. The problem is not so much not knowing what works, as not knowing how to deploy what works at the scale needed.

Conclusions

If a metropolitan strategy for reducing poverty were combined with intervention in the metropolitan housing market to offer more choice in low income housing location; better planning for metropolitan development, transportation, housing, and job location to remedy rather than further aggravate inner city conditions; and improvements in the livability and human development qualities of low income neighborhoods, the cumulative effect could make a startling difference. Perhaps the Twin Cities could become the place with the brainpower, leadership, and resources to do what no other United States city has done: break out of the life-destroying debilitation of the poverty and inner city cycle.

Chapter Five

Metropolitan Housing
Choice in the 1990s

A decent home and suitable living environment for
every American family.

Housing Act of 1949

One of the most important factors in the future well-being of the
central city, and particularly the inner city, is the metropolitan housing market. Permanent change in the future of the inner city
requires attention to this market. The metropolitan housing market
is not the initial cause of poverty, but it does concentrate low
income households and poverty into the inner city. That concentration and isolation breed further poverty. Given the role of the
housing market, regional housing policy should give a great deal of
attention to social and inner city problems. Likewise, successful
efforts to find lasting solutions to these problems must reckon with
the regional housing market tendencies to concentrate and isolate
low income people and social problems in the inner cities.

Other aspects of the social and inner city situation such as
education, health care, drugs, and crime cannot be ignored. However, work on these problems must reconnect individuals and
neighborhoods to the regional economy and opportunity. Whether
fixing houses, reforming the welfare system, or arresting people,
programs that do not make these connections will not achieve long-
term success. The regional housing market is the major cause of the
concentration and disconnection. Dealing with this market is central
to permanent solutions of other problems.

Given this viewpoint, these should be the priorities of a metropolitan housing strategy for the 1990s:

- Reduce the housing market as the major force in concentration, isolation, and disconnection of disadvantaged people
  and inner city neighborhoods from opportunity and the
  metropolitan economy.

- Carry out the housing part of a strategy to begin the reversal of the physical and social conditions of the inner portion of the central cities.

- Increase the supply and diversify locational choice of low income housing. Give priority to improving the quality of low income living circumstances in the inner city and to the quantity of low income living opportunities in outlying areas.

- Make living in publicly-supported housing transitional and an opportunity for developing household self-sufficiency.

- Preserve and upgrade the existing stock of central city housing and attempt to direct private and public investment toward this stock.

- Develop a regional housing strategy that is, among other things, an attempt to influence capital flows. Such a housing strategy would want to see an increase of investment in the existing housing stock and neighborhoods, particularly private investment in the inner parts of the region. This strategy would also require an increase in public and private investment in low income housing throughout the region, particularly publicly-supported investments in the outer parts of the region. The desired result would be more private money in the center and more public money in the outer areas.

Such a strategy would include market incentives to increase the rate of investment in the existing housing stock and challenge existing incentives that encourage new construction. These incentive changes are needed to ensure that the predicted reduction in demographic demand for housing results in significant moderation of new housing construction, not just continued underinvestment in and abandonment of the existing stock. This should be national policy as well and might be accomplished by underwriting a more favorable mortgage interest rate or tax deductibility differential for purchase, rehabilitation, and improvements to existing housing.

A regional housing strategy to increase housing choice and reduce social and economic isolation in the inner cities would need local, metropolitan, state, and private programs to greatly increase the rate of public attention to and investment in low income housing, particularly in the outer parts of the region, coordinated with job, transportation, and human service investment.

Another set of activities, programs, and incentives would be needed to increase the flow of private investment to housing in the central parts of the region. This would include upgrading the stock and improving the entire housing package, marketing and promotion, and financing as discussed in Chapter Seven. The housing package to be improved and marketed must be viewed as much more than the residential structure. The package also includes the physical and social neighborhood; public services with emphasis upon security, appearance and cleanliness, and public education; and market concerns such as social status and investment security.

All of these programs are related. For example, the livability and twenty-year revitalization programs developed in Minneapolis will improve the inner and central city housing packages. The positive marketplace response needed for such local programs to succeed will increase significantly if regional and national incentives to push private investment toward existing housing are put in place.

However, if this increase in private investment in inner city housing is not matched by an increased investment in low income housing throughout the region, the already inadequate supply of low income housing will decrease. This will be followed by low income household displacement. Eventually, socially and economically disconnecting neighborhood conditions will simply be pushed down to pop up elsewhere.

Housing programs frequently fail to reconcile, or even admit, the basic conflict between two goals: maintaining and revitalizing neighborhoods, and our de facto nationwide policy of providing low income housing by devaluing central city neighborhoods. Unless this conflict is addressed, neighborhood decline will win out in the inner cities.

That it is our de facto policy to provide low income housing through devaluing is no new insight. The common perception about the inner city, and of the poorly informed about the entire central city, is that the inner city is where low income people live and that is the way it is supposed to be. This is accompanied by the middle class perception that their own neighborhoods are where low income people do not live, and that if low income people move there, values (market and perhaps others) will decline.

If this common individual and societal understanding were expressed as public policy, the policy would state that we house low income people in bad neighborhoods in the central city and if more low income housing is needed, most of it will be provided through the decline of more city neighborhoods. This is an accurate description of the combined result of present public policy and the housing market. It is our de facto national housing policy.

Each time any level of government declares its intent to revitalize the inner city, it is in conflict with this policy. Any effort to revitalize neighborhoods and to better house low income people at the same time, without a concurrent increase in the supply and locational choice of low income housing, ignores the central, difficult issues.

The conflict between housing low income people and revitalizing neighborhoods can be reconciled only by some combination of the following:

1. Reducing the number of low income households by correcting the economic and social systems that produce these households.

2. Providing enough directed housing assistance to all low income households so they can compete in the private housing market at prices that will support housing and neighborhood maintenance and reinvestment.

3. Providing a permanent and sufficient supply of low income and social housing for all low income people at a level that meets not only their needs, but the standards the private marketplace demands and public policy wants.

Even in the case of fewer low income households and more households with more resources and choices, unsatisfactory areas may be abandoned as those choices are exercised. Those left behind would then be in an even more difficult situation unless adequate public social and housing investment were available to ameliorate the situation or prepare them to get out also.

These relationships and conflicts among investment, housing, social needs and people make it clear that neither the private marketplace nor the efforts of one city will ever be satisfactory. Only a coordinated city, metropolitan, state, and national housing strategy that recognizes inherent conflicts among housing goals can resolve these conflicts and keep the dynamics of the housing market from creating isolated and disconnected inner city neighborhoods.

Cities and suburbs have long influenced the housing market. Maintaining basic services, attending to security and sanitation, constructing and maintaining capital infrastructure, and providing park and school systems have the intent and effect of influencing the housing market, or at least of letting it play itself out over a place. Zoning and other development regulation is direct intervention in the market. Urban redevelopment is even greater involve- ment. Providing low income housing is participation in the housing market from both the supply and demand side, depending upon the program. The public is part of the metropolitan housing market in all sorts of ways.

And yet local, metropolitan, and state government do not attempt to fundamentally change the "big marketplace." Our activity is to prepare for it, react to it, provide for it, try to have a marketable product in it, and clean up after it. Metropolitan planning attempts to smooth out some of the rough edges and occasionally some of the social justice repercussions. It neither

redirects nor fundamentally changes how the market works. Only
the federal government, usually as an incidental result of economic
and fiscal policy, transportation programs, housing financing and
defense, has had significant impact upon the basic housing market.
Present shelter assistance for low income people is not a public
attempt to change the way the marketplace works, but to enter into
the marketplace as it stands on behalf of those unable to acquire
adequate shelter.

While most public involvement in the housing market is to
accommodate and serve it, there have been a few efforts to change
it. The most important of these are state and metropolitan in origin
and scope. Regional fair share plans have, in some cases, dealt with
the distribution of publicly assisted or non-market housing. But
they have more to do with accommodating than changing the metropolitan market. In some places, such as Oregon and Massachusetts,
state mandates require local governments to adopt plans and
ordinances that permit a reasonably full range of densities, styles,
and prices of housing to be built within their jurisdiction. This
method represents an active effort to change the marketplace, or
perhaps, an effort to restrain local government from obstructing and
excluding parts of the market from its communities.

Increasing Private Investment in the Existing Housing Stock

In the 1990s one of the most important statistics about the metropolitan housing market will be the difference between the number
of new units constructed and the number of new households. The
number of new households will be much reduced. The larger the
difference between new construction and real demand growth, the
more disinvestment and abandonment of the existing stock.

The demographic demand for new units will be positive, that
is, the total size of the needed housing stock will grow. Also, some
replacement construction will be needed. Therefore, there need not
be a glut or even an excess if there is some restraint in new construction. But there will be a much reduced demand, resulting in a
tug of war between the need of the development industry and outlying suburbs to keep building at previous rates and the need to
occupy and maintain an adequate rate of investment in the existing
stock. The consequences will be mostly felt in the older suburbs,
central cities, and inner city neighborhoods.

This situation means that a high priority in both metropolitan
and national housing policy must be to find ways to direct the
market and capital toward the existing housing stock. It requires
policy that recognizes and works to preserve the valuable resource
we have in existing urban land, infrastructure, and communities. At

the national level, it requires seeing that one way to increase investment in productivity and national competitiveness is to reduce, or at
least not promote, consumption expenditures. This can be accomplished by no longer using public policy to encourage over-
expenditure in new housing in some locations, far beyond shelter,
comfort or investment, while failing to provide basic shelter needs
in others.

The cities, as well as developed suburbs and the metropolitan
area, need to begin to develop national and state housing policy
legislation that favors investment in the existing housing stock.
Much of this concerns income tax policy and the deductibility of
mortgage interest. Reductions in the maximum amounts of deductibility would generally help existing housing, particularly if the
additional taxes generated were directed to low income housing or
financing home improvements.

We need additional national housing policy that underwrites a
more favorable interest rate or more favorable tax treatment on
loans to purchase or improve existing housing. Economic modeling
would be needed to determine effective rates and costs, but at some
rate differential it would change capital flows. To the extent that
improving existing housing is more labor intensive than is new construction, it would be a shift from resource consumption to use of
labor. While awaiting, or perhaps in addition to, this sort of national
housing policy, the Twin Cities should try metropolitan approaches
to shifting capital flows toward the existing housing stock.

Pilot programs could test the impact of favorable interest or tax
treatment. Development fees tied to higher-cost new construction
could be used to reduce excess construction and generate financing
that could perhaps be used for low income housing in the same
municipality. The Metropolitan Council could be the place to
research the metropolitan housing market and propose the incentives needed to push capital towards the existing housing stock.
This would improve the context and increase success of local
government and neighborhood efforts to maintain and revitalize
their communities.

Providing Choice in Low Income Housing

Maintaining a sufficient supply of low income housing at any location is a challenge. The arguments against investing available
funding in outlying low income housing are familiar: that low
income people are better off in the inner city, that this is the market
and funding that the central cities should keep for themselves, that
giving low income households the choice to leave the inner city
will lead to abandonment of the city, that low income people dis-
rupt suburban neighborhoods, that local suburban governments

have a right to sort by economic status, and that the necessary social and transportation services are not available in the suburbs and
difficult to deliver to decentralized locations.

If any of these arguments, particularly those about where low
income people want to live, have merit, efforts to increase the
supply and locational choice of low income housing should be con-
sumer demand responsive. Low income households are the
consumers. What consumers want and view as good for their own
households is best tested by giving them a real choice and good
information about that choice. Experience to date with suburban
low income housing says there is more demand for this housing
than the current supply.

The following summary of the housing stock shows that
publicly-assisted housing is a very small proportion of the total
Twin Cities housing stock.

Table 1. Distribution of Housing Units

Total housing units, 1986	843,000
Central cities	288,000
Suburban	555,000

Table 2. Location of Subsidized Housing Units

	1989	1980
Subsidized units	44,400	32,500
Central cities	25,500	20,300
Suburbs	18,900	12,200

Table 3. Type of Occupancy

	Mixed Use (Family)		Elderly	
	1989	1980	1989	1980
Central cities	12,100	8,600	13,400	11,700
Suburbs	10,900	7,100	8,000	5,100
Total	23,000	15,700	21,400	16,800

Table 4. Waiting Lists and Vacancies, Subsidized Housing

	Public Housing Vacancy Rate, 1989	Rental Assistance Waiting Lists, 1989
Central cities	5.9%	2,885
Suburbs	1.3%	7,534
Total		10,419

The data in these tables are from publications of the Twin Cities Metropolitan Council (*Looking Ahead At Housing*, September 1988, and *Changes In the Subsidized Housing Market, 1980- 1989*, March 1990).

Providing more locational choice should not replace working to rebuild inner city communities. The goal should be real metropolitan-scale choice of locations for low income households, as well as inner city communities encouraging people to stay there by choice, not because they are trapped there.

Private housing expenditures return high value because the household selects a location that gives it the package it wants. That may be some balance of proximity to jobs, services, friends, churches, or living within a preferred school district, open space amenities, community services—whatever that household deems important and is able to balance and afford. A public housing dollar, or a low income private dollar, that does not offer these choices buys less because it buys only shelter. More locational choice for low income housing consumers allows the marketplace to do for them what it does for others. Other ways in which the program should resemble the private market for market-rate housing is that it be capable of high volumes of activity, provide adequate public sector services, and be ensured a continuing supply of financing and public subsidy.

Concerns about provision of special services to dispersed low income housing should be addressed with the idea that service dependency is a temporary situation. Low income housing should be considered "opportunity housing," with a flexible set of social services, education, job training, and transportation possibilities tied to the housing unit or certificate. The goal should be household self-sufficiency within a reasonable time. The housing provision should be reasonably transitional; the primary purpose for providing the housing should be access to opportunities and, ultimately, self-sufficiency.

To a significant extent this housing would be occupied by single parents. The characteristics needed for successful single-parent family housing have been examined in detail by Cook, et al. (*Expanding Opportunities for Single Parents Through Housing,* Christine Cook, Mary Vogel-Heffernan, Barbara Lukermann, Sherrie Pugh, Esther Wattenberg, 1988). The Cook report deals with five aspects of single-parent housing: design, financing, management, location and neighborhood characteristics, and support services. Because one important criticism of dispersed low income housing is that it merely recreates ghetto-like conditions in suburban locations and that service provision is difficult, the neighborhood guidelines proposed by the report should be part of regional policy for low income housing. The report recommends that "appropriate neighborhoods for single parents must include these elements: 1) safety and security; 2) services; 3) opportunities for interaction with socioeconomically and demographically similar populations on the micro-scale and diverse populations on the macro-scale; 4) a surrounding neighborhood that is well-maintained; and 5) communities receptive to single-parent housing that are not themselves concentrations of vulnerable populations" (p. 9).

Those five neighborhood characteristics are not only guidelines for locating regional low income housing, they are qualities that much private and public low income housing in the inner cities fails to provide. In further recommending that this housing be provided in small developments and avoid concentrations of vulnerable populations, the report provides further guidance on how to proceed. The level of detail provided on subjects from transportation access to design to supporting social services answers most questions and objections about low income housing location and provision.

All of the essential social services are universally available through the existing county, metropolitan, state, school district and private providers of such services. Decentralization is more a matter of management and innovation in delivering services than new organization. Also, a metropolitan plan could exclude areas that are difficult to serve, if the excluded areas contribute to regional housing fund resources to be applied to the program in other places.

Neither the cities nor the suburbs should be concerned about a program of choice in the location of transitional low income housing, given where new jobs and market-rate housing are locating. Metropolitan Council forecasts show the central city share of metropolitan jobs declining from 44 to 34 percent and the developing suburban share increasing from 21 to 30 percent between 1980 and 2000. Only 20,000 of the total job growth of 336,000 is forecast to be central city (*Looking Ahead At Housing,* Metropolitan Council, 1988). Only 13,000 of the 209,000 growth in households between 1980 and 2000 are expected to locate in the central cities.

Low income households must be able to move with job and housing development. Anything that traps them in the inner city while job growth is mostly suburban will deepen economic disconnection.

Will large-scale suburban low income housing programs weaken inner city communities? It is frequently observed that one cause of recent worsening of inner city conditions is the loss of middle and upper income economic and community leaders and success models who have moved to more affluent neighborhoods. A large-scale housing program that focused on those of moderate income might continue this trend, leaving behind concentrations of the most disadvantaged. A choice in housing location program should include low as well as moderate income. It has been proven that public housing residents can improve their circumstances in suburban locations.

A large-scale suburban low income housing program could be viewed as diffusing low income and/or minority political power. There are clear cases in U.S. cities of large-scale public policy in urban renewal, highway construction, and annexation where programs touted for the economic or social good of the larger community had the result, and sometimes the intent, of weakening minority communities and their political strength.

The premise of this report is that a program of choice in low income housing is needed at the household level, to improve access to jobs and other opportunities. Perhaps this approach places individual choice above the existing community. Debate over whether and how to start housing programs should look hard at the impact upon the community and political structure. I would suggest the appropriate choice centers not on political structure but on what is best for children.

The long-range proposal here is that a low income household have as much opportunity to locate throughout the metropolitan area as within the inner city. We need choice in low income housing, just as we have in schools and market-rate housing. Choice in housing location carries with it choices of schools, job proximity, type and quality of public services, kind of neighborhood, and the entire set of opportunities that come with housing location. Narrowing that choice to inner city locations represents a dramatic limitation. The societal cost of continuing that limitation is greater than the cost of change.

A great deal of change is needed, with a limited amount of resources. Providing housing subsidy only in the inner city changes only the shelter condition. Offering a choice to the entire metropolitan area establishes the opportunity for a family to change a whole set of circumstances for essentially the same public cost.

Given an adequate and distributed supply, there is probably a demand for many thousands of units of suburban low income family housing at approximately present levels of subsidy. However, we won't know unless we begin to increase the supply through a market-like demand situation in which an incremental number of units are added each year for as long as the demand continues. If it turns out that low income households begin not to choose suburban locations and prefer the inner city, or if and when the demand for units is met, we would stop adding outlying units and focus resources on the central cities.

There is certainly enough demand to carry a program for several years. A reasonable scale, though much less than the regional low income housing need, would be a program that would provide at least 20,000 units if continued for ten years (2,000 per year). If we were very successful in creating the opportunity housing concept described above, turnover would be more rapid and aggregate need would be reduced.

Two thousand units per year would translate into an average of forty units per year within fifty municipalities. By the year 2000, this rate of activity would accumulate to only about 2.2 percent of the metropolitan housing supply, but would more than double the total regional supply of family subsidized housing if existing units were held, and more than triple the present suburban supply. The total regional supply of all subsidized housing would rise from 44,000 to 64,000, just over 6 percent of the forecast total housing stock of 960,000 and around two-thirds of 1985 estimated needs (*Looking Ahead at Housing*, Metropolitan Council, 1988).

The regional distribution would be about one-third central city and two-thirds suburban, with the suburbs still having less than a proportionate share based upon population distribution.

The central cities' response to this should be to be as competitive as possible in both the market-rate and low income housing markets. In the low income or public market, the central cities would need to improve inner city conditions sufficiently to convince low income households with the choice of leaving to decide to stay.

This kind of large-scale low income housing effort might be more feasible in the 1990s if the national predicted labor shortage results in shortages in the suburbs. This shortage should provide increased resources to low income families to whom the jobs can be made accessible. Also, to the perhaps limited extent that supplying the demand is a matter of constructing new units, the development sector will be looking for opportunities to counteract the downturn in housing demand, and could be supportive.

The cost of this program would be high because it should include low and very low income households. It should be a shared effort of nonprofit, national, state, metropolitan, and local funding. As in Florida, and some other places, the program should seek to use, but not depend upon, federal funding. To whatever extent creative revision of zoning and development codes, building practices, financing, reducing management and profit overhead, or other means can bring units closer to low income affordability, costs can be reduced.

The search for funding should begin at the federal level because it is within our national economic and social system that disadvantaged and low income situations are produced. Also, this sort of program is needed on a national level. While there is a lot more creativity in housing at the state and local than the federal level, the sum of this state and local effort does not approach the scale of the national program needed.

An approximately $50 billion per year national home ownership program is now in place through mortgage interest income tax deductibility. The sum of these deductions reduces annual tax collections by about $50 billion. To the extent that this incentive stimulates housing investment beyond shelter needs, it encourages use of national capital for consumption that might be better invested in national economic productivity. If we care as much about economic strength as current discussions about productivity, global competitiveness, and capital gains taxation suggest, we should try to reduce rather than encourage excess consumption of housing. Limiting the interest deductibility on mortgages of $150,000 or $200,000 or less would begin to reduce reliance on consumption as national economic policy. It would also increase federal revenues that could be targeted directly to more basic housing. If one believes that strong metropolitan areas are part of global economic competitiveness, reinvesting this revenue to help break down the isolation, disconnection and economic difficulties of low income people and inner cities would represent a shift of investment from consumption to national economic development.

To the extent that state income tax policy follows federal, it would seem that reducing deductibility would also produce state revenues. A potential new source of state revenue would also come about. A metropolitan sales tax for transit is currently under discussion. This may be a good idea. However, before such an important new tax policy is put in place and directed to a particular use, a discussion of the comparative long-range value of other uses should take place. Perhaps the sales tax should be applied to both low income housing and transit, with the transit system staged and located to support decentralized low income housing location.

Existing home sales in the metropolitan area range from 20,000 to over 30,000 units per year. New homes sales have been averaging over 20,000 units per year, but are expected to decline. If total new and existing sales were 40,000 units per year at an average value of $80,000, total volume would be $3.2 billion per year. A 1 percent sales tax on this level of sales would produce $32 million in annual revenues, but would probably be somewhat regressive and might overlap other taxes. It could be made less regressive through a sliding scale ranging from one-half to 2 percent. If this resulted in $20 million per year, that would cover a one-time cost write-down of $10,000 per unit on 2,000 units each year or $20,000 on 1,000 units. It would alternatively provide a continuing rent subsidy of $300 per month for 5,500 units. It could be the core of a significant program if subsidized by federal and local government support and private sources.

In those communities that continue to have new housing development, development fees to cover the cost of low income housing in that community might be considered. A state-collected luxury tax on very expensive new housing, over $250,000 perhaps, to be applied to low income housing in the community of collection might be considered. In the absence of a metropolitan sales tax, local sales tax might be permitted by state law. Some means of local support would be needed.

The point of this brief analysis is only to suggest that a program of this magnitude is not inconceivable. Cost is a challenge, but resources are available. The long-term benefits would be at least as great, and probably much greater, than those of light rail transit system, and the cost would be less.

Conclusions

It is, as always, a matter of where to apply our rather considerable private and public resources in equitable and productive ways. Public investment applied effectively to useful programs is as critical as private investment to economic growth. Public investment that represents real economic development by setting the stage and clearing the obstacles to long-range economic growth is a necessary spur to metropolitan, state, and national competitiveness. A program designed to get at the serious loss of economic resources represented by inadequate shelter, and the continuing isolation and disconnection of low income households from the metropolitan economy, deserve a share of our resources.

It is clear that intervention in the metropolitan housing market dynamics is essential to reducing the spread of inner city blight to the rest of the city. There is also clearly a demand for geographically dispersed low income housing that far exceeds the present supply. Research shows that those low income households with locational choice, somewhat like private market housing, do better in employment and education. The oft-cited arguments to the contrary are inaccurate. Social services can be adjusted and tied to the housing subsidy. Though expensive, a much larger choice in housing programs is affordable. It is essential to gain access to new job growth. It is an essential part of a metropolitan inner city strategy.

Chapter Six

Improving the Livability and Human Development Characteristics of Low Income Neighborhoods

> This morning—like almost every morning these days—there were more little coffins than big ones.
> It's a trend that has recently become noticeable. Last year, the number of children buried on Hart Island was 42 percent higher than only three years earlier.
>
> Minneapolis *Star Tribune*, December 12, 1990, p. 1.

For the foreseeable future there will be concentrations of low income and poverty households in the inner portions of the central cities. Poverty will continue to exist, older inner city housing will offer relatively cheap shelter, the dynamics of the metropolitan housing market will continue to concentrate low income households, and the societal housing policy of providing low income shelter by devaluing inner city neighborhoods will continue.

The causes and solutions to much of the inner city poverty situation are larger than the central city. City leadership needs to work with metropolitan leadership, and the larger society, to reduce the incidence of poverty and its concentration in the inner city, and to reconnect isolated city neighborhoods with the metropolitan economy. However, even if the structural causes of poverty are addressed aggressively and successfully, improvements will be gradual and incomplete. This means the city will need to continue long-term efforts to keep as much of itself as possible marketable in the metropolitan market, and to maintain the livability and human development characteristics of its inner city neighborhoods.

Maintaining the market strength of most neighborhoods is necessary for community strength, a tax base to provide services and amenities for all residents, market support for a retail and commercial network for all residents, institutional strength, diversity.

Most important, it limits the degree of isolation of low income and poverty households and neighborhoods. This will be discussed more fully in a later chapter.

However, whatever the outcome of efforts to work on the larger picture, the city as a community must deal with one aspect of this situation itself. That is the quality of living in the inner city and whether and to what degree being a resident (short-term, long-term or born there) of an inner city neighborhood becomes a cause of further reduction in life chances. Can we keep poverty neighborhoods from being a breeding ground of further poverty? How?

As with the metropolitan housing market, conditions in low income neighborhoods may not be an initial or root cause of poverty. However, just as the housing market concentrates poverty and that concentration becomes a cause of further poverty, resulting neighborhood conditions become a cause of further poverty.

Within an overall city and metropolitan strategy to deal with inner city problems, the city's primary role is to deal effectively with the difficult conditions caused by poverty concentrations. The city must make living in low income areas as nondebilitating and noncontagious as possible; it must provide a setting in which there is opportunity for people to improve their lives.

In these conditions, *improving the human development characteristics* is more important than trying to revitalize the neighborhood in a marketplace sense, or at least must precede it. This is true because people are more important than houses, but even if the long-range goal is marketplace revitalization, it won't be achievable until deficiencies in education, public safety, public health, and general public conditions are dealt with. Factors that severely affect the basic livability of a place effectively remove it from the metropolitan housing marketplace.

Whether marketplace revitalization should eventually become the goal also depends upon whether there is a financed program to assist the low income households that will otherwise be displaced by the higher prices inherent in increased market strength. Either way, the process must begin by improving basic livability. That is a key city and community responsibility for a number of reasons.

First, much of the work needed falls within the traditional city functions of public safety, public health, education, and maintaining overall neighborhood conditions.

Second, failure to maintain these traditional services and other aspects of livability is a clear factor in the city decline pattern that has preceded us. Not letting this happen is one way to stop digging the hole.

Third, the quality of life in inner city neighborhoods is critical to the future of the rest of the city. The better the conditions within our most difficult neighborhoods, the less negative impact they have upon surrounding areas, upon the image of the entire city as a place to live and the strength of all city neighborhoods in the metropolitan housing market. There is a strong tendency for the real estate market to oversimplify and view inner city conditions as representative of the entire central city. When we improve conditions and reduce bad news about the inner city, we are strengthening all of our neighborhoods and inner ring suburbs.

Fourth, to persuade metropolitan leadership and others to contribute to an overall inner city strategy, the city must be clear about what it intends to do itself.

This is a real challenge, both to think about and to carry out. It requires thinking about neighborhoods in ways different from, or in addition to, physical and housing conditions. It requires giving first attention to the human development characteristics of neighborhoods.

The Human Development Characteristics of Neighborhoods

To clarify what might be meant by the human development characteristics of a neighborhood, the following discussion focuses on various ways to analyze those qualities, to help clarify what essential human development characteristics might be, and how they might lead to different ways of thinking about neighborhoods. It analyzes different approaches to deciding how well people are doing and whether their neighborhood is aiding or injuring their well-being.

The following discussion covers first a complex comprehensive statistical approach, then simpler ways of looking at only the most indicative variables, and finally a more subjective approach focusing on the well-being of children as the most telling indicator of neighborhood success.

A comprehensive statistical approach to analyzing the human development strength of a place might have categories for mortality and survival, health and security, hope and potential, physical economic conditions, and opportunity. The actual data used would not be much different than that now used, but the arrangement will reveal much more (Figure 8).

The mortality and survival category suggests (as does common sense) that survival is a necessary condition for doing well. If infant mortality rates, homicide rates, suicide rates, and life expectancy were analyzed by place, some rather harsh differences might be revealed. They would tell a lot about the loss of livability and human development potential in some neighborhoods.

Figure 8. Building Blocks of Successful Neighborhoods

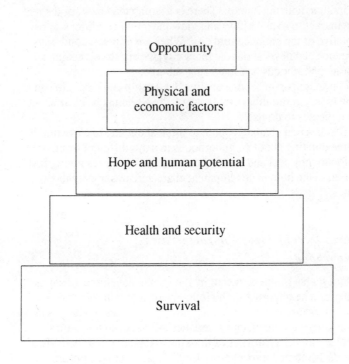

The public safety and public health category would include thinking about rates of important but less severe conditions than those above. Measures such as prenatal care, nutrition, health care availability and use, assaults, drug arrests, fires, accident rates, and other indicators of health and security situations that would impede successful living are needed here.

The hope and potential category would focus on the presence or absence of vital family and community support for human development and availability and use of organizations, institutions, and services. This might include measures of preschool use; public or private school enrollment and success; truancy; availability and use of other community institutions such as city parks, churches, YMCAs, ethnic organizations; and other measures designed to indicate neighborhood access to and use of community services to prepare for successful living.

The physical and economic conditions category would include the usual statistics about employment, income, shelter conditions, general neighborhood conditions, and other traditional indicators of neighborhood quality.

The opportunity category includes such things as higher education attendance and completion, long-term and career employment with benefits and advancement opportunity, business ownership, home equity and ownership, retirement plans, things that are a little closer to "the good life."

These examples are so loaded with traditional middle class values that they may not be appropriate indicators of opportunity. But that is the society in which most Americans are preparing or hoping to succeed. In any case, the question is to what degree the neighborhood is a place of opportunity beyond survival and getting by, where people can develop and apply their human potential.

A simpler approach to considering neighborhood strengths and weaknesses might be to apply Isabel Sawhill's conclusions that the "root causes" of persistent poverty are weak families, substantial joblessness and poor education ("Poverty and the Underclass," in *Challenge to Leadership*, The Urban Institute, 1988, Isabel Sawhill, ed., 231). A set of statistics to indicate concentrations of these "root causes" would reveal neighborhoods with poor human development characteristics.

Another approach would apply four indicators developed by The Urban Institute (also Sawhill), intended to look beyond income to reveal persistent underclass problems and poverty-impacted neighborhoods. These indicators are welfare dependency, adult male joblessness, premature school leaving, and single-parent households. William Julius Wilson also considers adult male joblessness due to structural and geographic changes in the economy as a basic cause and indicator of single-parent households and poverty conditions.

As shown in Chapter Two, concentrations of these four and other conditions have increased steadily for several decades in portions of the Twin Cities' inner cities. Use of these or similar indicators would reveal those places of weak human development characteristics and, more importantly, lead to thinking about people-oriented strategies for those places. As one moves through cities, the areas in which the most severe conditions are highly concentrated are easily visible and clearly different from other low income areas, perhaps most clearly by the street presence of adult males.

If one agrees, as this report does, with the William Julius Wilson thesis that a basic cause of continuing inner city poverty is cultural isolation, measures of the human development qualities of neighborhoods should include some that indicate the degree and nature of that isolation. However, most of the research work on isolation ends up implying, but not actually proving, the condition.

Objective measures that might tell how connected or isolated households in a neighborhood are from the larger metropolitan economy and opportunity have not, to my knowledge, been applied at any scale. Location of employment and travel patterns would be measures of a sort. It is my belief that the cultural isolation of some neighborhoods can be easily seen, and that such isolation is a key weakness in the human development potential of these places.

A more positive approach would be to look for the capacities of a place rather than the deficiencies. John McKnight's thesis is that we spend too much time listing negatives and should instead look for the internal human capabilities that can be mobilized to strengthen the community.

A successful neighborhood is one in which people can lead or prepare for successful lives. It is one that provides the community setting and development support that individuals and families (whether average or with special situations) need for successful lives. An unsuccessful community is one that cannot or does not provide this setting and support and detracts from rather than contributes to successful living.

This is related to self-sufficiency, of both people and neighborhoods. Self-sufficiency is not the ability to live without any connection to others. This does not occur in any urban society. Even the most wealthy, healthy, wise and independent are, in fact, dependent upon collaboration with others for national defense, educating their neighbors if not themselves, roads, traffic signals, and a good deal more. They are also dependent upon the marketplace for income. The marketplace or economy, in turn, depends upon society and government to provide the systems and stability needed for its orderly operation.

Self-sufficiency in a complex society means the ability of an individual, family, or community to live with some success within the interdependent socioeconomic and political conditions that exist, with some ability to collaborate to change those conditions. No one is born with that self-sufficiency. Certain needs must be met. Someone must nurture, shelter, teach, educate, train, finance, assist, mentor.

Those things that the individual cannot do for oneself must be provided or assisted by another. What cannot be accomplished by the individual, family, or informal structure at one level of aggregation will either not occur or must be carried out at some higher level of aggregation. If not available at the next level, the need will pass through to more complex organizations. Eventually there will be some sort of action, perhaps remedial and supportive or perhaps isolating and punishing, to deal with either the initial condition or its later, more difficult manifestation.

So perhaps when we think about the human development qualities of a neighborhood, we should consider how well individuals and families are doing and then how those needs that cannot be met by the individual or family are responded to in the community. Are the schools, recreation, and other human development services there not only for the typical and normal situation, but for the unique, more difficult, and less well-prepared? Is what can't be done by one level recognized and dealt with by the next?

For example, there is clearly an epidemic of children in inner city areas who are under- or un-parented. Children's success in life will partially depend upon their own strength, spirit, and compensating abilities. However, there will be some dependence upon others for support and development to overcome the disadvantage of under-parenting. A caring, competent and stable immediate family can provide or purchase much of what is needed to develop potential or overcome handicaps. But the special needs of under-parented children will immediately move outward to some form of community or governmental responsibility.

The situation can be ignored. But a more difficult and painful circumstance of some sort will evolve. The need will pass through each level that cannot or does not deal with it until something is done. What is finally done may be humane or inhumane; may be done by the community, some institution at some level of government, or prison, but eventually, at some level of collaboration, some action will be taken. It will almost always be true that earlier remedial intervention at the community level would have enhanced human potential, and would have been less costly to society than later, perhaps harsher remedies at higher levels of government. Headstart will prevent more crime than will crime prevention programs. Crime prevention programs will bring more justice than will criminal justice systems. More concern for justice will provide more public safety than will prisons and other public safety programs.

On the other hand, a community may enhance people's lives, providing support and opportunity for human development, but may look quite squalid from the viewpoint of traditional physical analysis and other norms. If people are living and preparing to live successful lives, the neighborhood is successful, notwithstanding its physical conditions.

Perhaps the most telling questions about a neighborhood, and questions that do not require mountains of statistics and analysts, are these: Are the children living here as likely as those living elsewhere to have successful lives? Are neighborhood conditions improving or decreasing that likelihood? Why or why not?

These are questions that an individual observer can ask and probably answer somewhat accurately, though with some risk of stereotyping. Residents' answers to these questions would be quite accurate. These straightforward questions about how children are doing can shortcut a lot of analysis and cut through a lot of confusion about neighborhood strategies. An answer that is clearly "yes, they will do well and the neighborhood is an asset and not a liability to these children's life chances" indicates much about the place. "No, and the neighborhood is making it even worse" tells as much. "Why not?" could stimulate preparation of an agenda for neighborhood improvement that would address the most important issue, though not necessarily be restricted to the well-being of children. The improvement agenda could range from employment for adult males to smaller class sizes. How well children are doing is not only critical in its own right, but is a surrogate indicator for the most important aspects of quality in most neighborhoods.

In the most difficult places, housing or neighborhood revitalization is not first on the agenda, or second or third. Success should not first be measured by whether the neighborhood achieves physically better conditions or whether the housing becomes more marketable. Physical condition and housing condition are issues to the extent that poor shelter or neighborhood environment are a burden to successful coping, staying healthy, getting educated, or staying employed. For example, removing lead poisoning hazards might be a higher housing priority than total rehabilitation. Otherwise, more basic programs should come first.

To further explain this point of view, the usual situation in declining neighborhoods is that the turnover of residents begins to be a pattern of transfer from those better off financially to those less so, and perhaps a decline in the economic fortunes of those not moving. Eventually, there are inadequate resources to maintain physical conditions, services decline, and the process spirals downward.

A revitalizing neighborhood is one in which the reverse is true, one that is holding or increasing its strength in the metropolitan housing marketplace and turnover pattern is toward more affluent residents. And while such revitalizing is usually viewed as good by realtors, existing property owners, new and some old residents and planners, it also means less housing for low income people. This is a fundamental conflict between goals for revitalizing neighborhoods and the present national and metropolitan housing policy that envisions providing low income housing by devaluing city neighborhoods.

This marketplace and policy conflict can only be resolved through some combination of less poverty, more housing reserved for low income, and enough housing support for low income households to maintain neighborhood market strength. Because these conditions are not now in place, in some neighborhoods great care must be taken to deal with the people situations rather than seeking only marketplace revitalization that might, in fact, force residents out.

In such places attention must first be given to restoring service quality and human livability, then to how low income people are going to be economically empowered and/or housed. If these situations are successfully resolved, marketplace revitalization becomes appropriate and possible.

Ways of analyzing and considering these human development characteristics range from complex to quite straightforward. The intent was to think about neighborhoods in more people-oriented and less physical terms than is usually the case, and set the stage to improve the life chances of those living in the most difficult places.

Strategies for Improving the Livability and Human Development Characteristics of Inner City Neighborhoods

The less locational choice available for low income households, the more critical it is that the neighborhoods in which they must live be safe, clean, healthy and supportive. Knowing how to achieve acceptable conditions in a given neighborhood requires attention to the specific situation and service organizations that are flexible. While security, health issues, neighborhood appearance and sanitation, and education are clearly a major part of maintaining livability, the relative emphasis upon each of these and other services must be flexible.

Why do general public service results deteriorate in low income and poverty areas? Partly because that's what we expect. We know or expect that low income people are more likely to live in insecure areas and to become victims of crime; that increased rental and reduced owner-occupancy of housing will reduce care of both house and surroundings; that children will be less prepared for school and have more health problems; that the troubled and the troublesome will concentrate in low income areas; that trouble will breed trouble.

In fact, conditions do become more difficult and services more difficult to provide. Given the larger situation, decline may be inevitable. What is not necessarily inevitable, but very much expected, is that service results will also deteriorate as the challenge increases. We expect less security, less school success, poorer appearance and sanitation, and an overall less healthy environment in poor neighborhoods. We don't expect children there to have the same life chances as in other places.

Increasing tolerance and acceptance of inferior results in traditional municipal services such as education, public safety, public health, general appearance and sanitation is the path that cities follow to failure of these services. The resulting intolerable conditions not only jeopardize immediate residents and feed the "cycle of poverty," but eventually destroy the image and condition of the entire city.

The failure is often seen as failure of the residents themselves. That may be partly accurate, but a good deal of the failure is failure of service delivery systems. We don't expect to achieve good results in difficult areas. And we don't. This expectation and acceptance of poor results is clear from lack of general public outcry over school dropout rates of 50 or 75 percent in some low income areas, increasing rather than decreasing infant mortality, increased homicide rates, and unsafe streets.

The remedial programs proposed to correct these conditions are usually seen as some combination of housing, economic development and social services, the standard tools of community development and human service agencies traditionally assigned to solve the problem. These are often the wrong tools.

Improving inner city conditions is first very much about traditional "health, safety, and welfare" kinds of services; the basic municipal and community services such as utilities, public safety, public works, public health, and education. Those providing these services must be willing to innovate, adjust methods, and apply resources to achieve essentially the same quality results as in more conventional and less difficult situations. This is a pivotal point of view. Partnerships in community policing, cooperative neighborhood sweeps to locate and remedy environmental conditions, organizing, and community building efforts all fit the idea of results-oriented innovation in service delivery.

Headstart and other forms of preschool education to overcome under-parenting of low income children, smaller class sizes, financial access to higher education to compensate for poverty situations fit this philosophy. When all else is failing, access to effective education is the necessary condition for individuals to prepare themselves to either improve the place or find a better place for the next generation.

This sort of results-oriented service approach for maintaining livability and human development potential needs to be considered as a basic strategy in inner city neighborhoods. This is often thought of as a matter of more emphasis upon social services in low income areas, but it is also a matter of how more traditional municipal services are delivered and the expectations for quality results.

To avoid weakening inner city communities, any metropolitan housing program should be well-distributed among income levels, including the very poor. This, of course, reduces political and financial acceptability. It is clear from practice and research that suburban housing for former inner city public housing residences can be provided and can result in improved employment and educational success. To the extent that a social network remains between those moving and those remaining, some improved information about employment, education, and residential opportunity might flow back to the inner city community and reduce isolation.

As discussed in Chapter Five, dispersed low income housing needs to be done in ways that do not cause isolation. It must be opportunity-oriented and transitional rather than permanent. It seems, in the long run, that all neighborhoods will be stronger when those who live there are at least partially there by choice. It is, however, unlikely that a program of large enough scale to end the housing market concentration of low income in the inner city will be put in place soon. Therefore, it is not inconsistent to advocate, simultaneously, both metropolitan-scale choice in low income housing location programs, and programs to build and improve community conditions in the inner city.

Neither of the opposite choices is viable. To lock low income people into the inner city when job growth is almost entirely suburban is to guarantee long-term deepening of problems. To accept existing inner city conditions and await metropolitan-wide improvement will do likewise. Both dispersal of housing location choices and building an inner city community must be pursued.

It seems clear that improving the human development characteristics of a neighborhood requires innovations in organizing services delivery to see the finer grain of what is happening to people, and how to respond more precisely.

The isolation that develops in low income areas is not just isolation of the neighborhood from the larger community, economy and opportunity, but also of individuals and households from one another and the community. Community building is partially working on this isolation on the neighborhood level.

Looking at community organization, John McKnight's approach, which emphasizes the positive aspects of a community and seeks to mobilize the capabilities of residents as the key resource, may not work, but neither have other efforts. His may be a better starting place than a needs study as a list of negatives. If one believes that a vital development component of a place is its sense of community and that individual life chances are enhanced by community strength and vice versa, then his models should be examined.

A community developing and implementing an innovative public safety program that uses the capabilities of residents has results beyond improved security. It develops the skill and organization to go to work on an employment strategy, education program, new park, or whatever the next agenda item may be. It develops residents' capabilities to respond to both community and individual situations.

McKnight's fundamental argument seems to be that low income areas have become places where consumption of services from professional providers has replaced individual and community productivity as the norm and that reversing that situation by using resident capabilities rather than public services only is the key to successful community building. In its fullest development, the McKnight approach would require unusual openness and flexibility on the part of traditional service providers. McKnight advocates replacing services and associated budgets with programs that direct the same money to residents to build the economic strength of the place.

Whether using some part of McKnight's approach or not, some form of community organization that becomes skilled at looking inside the place, at seeing opportunities and problems and remedies at a finer grain of detail, would be a necessary part of a strategy to improve the living conditions and human development characteristics of neighborhoods. This is clearly not the job of a community development organization in the traditional sense. The mission and work programs are quite different, though not necessarily incompatible.

This in place, the larger institutions would need to flexibly respond to what the community organization sees as the way to proceed. Thus, there are several challenges here. The first is developing and agreeing upon a community strategy that is precise, accurate and effective. The next is getting service providers to change their ideas sufficiently to let it happen. Third, if the service providers are to take the risk of changing themselves in the volatile and blaming public environment, some of the accountability, responsibility, and risk of failure must be shifted to the community.

There is, of course, a role for social services in remedying the human development weaknesses of a neighborhood, though as traditionally delivered, they are not what this approach is about. Perhaps there is a way to combine, in a demonstration neighborhood, a results-oriented city service strategy; less traditional social services delivery means, such as family resource centers or housing assistance connected to self-sufficiency programs; and a different approach to welfare, such as Minnesota's new Family Investment Program, with its emphasis on blending assistance and incentives for building self-sufficiency.

While traditional services, community organizing, and social services may have higher priority than housing, shelter plays a vital role in any successful neighborhood. Traditional municipal inspections must ensure a safe and sanitary standard for the entire low income area. This must precede use of limited resources to provide a few perfect units for a few families. It is possible, and probably useful, for misplaced, project-focused strategies to repeatedly produce annual statistics showing results and improvement in the form of attractive new projects and some totally rehabilitated units, while the real situation continues to get worse.

Public housing policy that uses public funds to locate low income households in areas where basic standards of safety, sanitation, and general public services are not met should be reexamined. Perhaps an opposite policy should be considered in which communities and cities either find ways to maintain quality service results that do not jeopardize life chances, or public housing resources should be used to help people get out of the neighborhood.

This does not mean that some places will be written off. It means that where the initial conditions are more difficult, the human development, livability, and public service conditions must be dealt with first. This is where the real failure occurs. Revitalization focusing only on housing and physical conditions won't work until basic livability is improved.

A recent newspaper story about the failure of the criminal justice system in Philadelphia reminded me of a conversation I once had with a Philadelphia city official. He said, essentially, that he hoped no one ever asked what happened to the "billion dollars." Elaboration revealed that the cumulative expenditure of fifteen years of community development block grant (CDBG) funds on housing was approaching one billion dollars in that city and it was hard to show much result. We both agreed that had either of us been asked fifteen years ago whether one billion dollars would do the job, we would have been sure it would. It didn't. Abandonment has risen sharply, depopulation continues, and social problems abound.

Housing expenditures will not repair the housing stock, restore the housing market, or rebuild communities in a city where a basic service, in this case the criminal justice system and public safety, is failing. The same applies to neighborhood revitalization.

To oversimplify, this means that only where the house is "worse" than the neighborhood conditions will money spent on its removal or rehabilitation pay off. If basic public conditions are continually improved, the proportion of the housing stock that may justify physical improvement beyond basic livability will increase at the same pace. Learning to adjust effort and expenditures between housing investment and improving general neighborhood conditions, to maintain a steadily improving balance, is strategically essential.

Conclusions

The less choice there is in the metropolitan housing market for low income people, the more critical it is that the inner city areas in which they must live be livable. Restoring the human development qualities of these places must be the first step in revitalization.

Low income neighborhoods are the convergence of the socioeconomic situations that create poverty, metropolitan housing markets and societal housing policy that concentrates that poverty into the inner city, and a number of metropolitan-scale policy and development patterns that further reinforce that concentration.

Revitalization of these neighborhoods is a long-term challenge. Until larger scale social and economic forces are improved, low income neighborhoods will occur somewhere. People need shelter. Present societal shelter policy is that most urban low income housing will be provided by the economic devaluation of inner city neighborhoods. Working to change all of these structural conditions must be part of a city and metropolitan inner city strategy.

In the meantime, regardless of the long-range goal, city and community, the process needs to start with things as they are and proceed systematically. This is the case even if the long-range goal is to restore the economic housing market and gentrify the area. It is also true because the chaos resulting from destroyed livability spreads the conditions to surrounding areas and the resulting "bad news" hurts the marketability of the entire city. However, the primary reason is that this is the key opportunity for the city and community to interrupt the "cycle of poverty" and keep inner city areas from further reducing life chances for disadvantaged people.

Since almost all job growth is suburban, locking poverty households into the inner city is a sure road to more problems in the future. Not giving low income people the same chance to choose a package of schools, services, neighbors, and proximity to work as others have, diminishes the value of housing assistance dollars.

We must learn to look at places from a human development point of view. This might be done with the complex statistical analysis that measures a place, from its basic survivability to its opportunity enhancement characteristics. It could be done by straightforward answers to questions like "How are children doing here, and are neighborhood and service conditions improving or hurting their life chances?" Why not? What now?

Where the revitalization process should begin depends upon the outcome of such examination and questioning. How much has been lost? How much strength and capacity remain? Has only marketplace strength been lost? Or is it becoming a place lacking in opportunity for the "good life." Has genuine physical and economic slippage begun? Has there been a loss of supportive community, of hope, expectations, preparation and education for successful lives? Are basic public safety and public health failing? Is staying alive becoming more difficult?

Following this thought process, the appropriate remedies depend upon how far down this list we had to go to reach an accurate "no" rather than upon the skills, favorite tools and habits of traditional human service and community development agencies, housing providers, planning departments, and political bodies. Revitalization must begin where the problem is.

Automatic assignment of the problem to community development agencies focused on housing and economic development programs often results in use of the wrong tools. Some form of community organization and process is needed that builds both community and individual strengths and uses existing resident capacities. Service providers must then learn to respond to the plans of these organizations. The communities and traditional providers must both share and accept responsibility, consequences, kudos and boos.

If, in addition, adequate policy is in place about how low income persons are to be housed, traditional revitalization can proceed without displacing low income households and just pushing people and problems to another place.

When these things have been done well and the human development qualities are maintained or restored, we can proceed with a much more effective use of resources, more likelihood of success and with confidence that the most important goal—improving the well-being and life chances of people—has been given priority.

Chapter Seven

Upgrading City Neighborhoods in the Metropolitan Housing Market

> The core of the community turns out to be the group
> that is anchored there at any given time by the
> buildings and by fixed commitment and affection.
> That group has to provide the current of continuity
> in the turbulent demographic stream. And it is that
> group, at any given time and place, who creates the
> framework for dealing with problems of growth and
> decline.
>
> John R. Borchert, 1987, p. 163.

A thriving city neighborhood is a valuable resource. It contains within it the long-term accumulation of human lives, time, spirit, labor, talent and capital. The accumulated value includes the physical and visible elements of streets, buildings, parks, utilities, trees; the less visible service, travel, market and employment patterns; the social relationships and networks; the special individual and community values and choices unique to the place.

If one moves through a thriving neighborhood, the physical evidence of the economic and emotional value residents and others give the place is easily seen. Painted houses, home improvements, "For Sale" and "Sold" signs, flower gardens and landscaping, shoveled walks, playgrounds, church congregations, children entrusted to the streets. Something is going on here that is valued in economic, social, and emotional ways. Granted that in modern society much of the traditional "neighborliness" is no longer present, there is still a valued human process playing out here.

The tangible components alone have a financial value impressive even in the age of big numbers. Three thousand housing units with an average value of $80,000 is $240 million, say one-quarter of a billion dollars. Add replacement costs of streets, pipes, trees, parks, churches, public and commercial buildings, and the sum would easily exceed $500 million—one-half billion dollars, that just the engineering side of life has invested in tangible structures.

This is without even attempting to quantify the intangible markets, social patterns, individual values, the accumulated choices that make up the even more valuable "community." To put it in economic terms, it would not be an exaggeration to describe a thriving functioning neighborhood as a billion dollar place.

Most concerns of central city living and governing are directly or indirectly related to changes in the relative value of these neighborhoods in the metropolitan marketplace. The difficulties of keeping or replacing retail business downtown and in older commercial strips and neighborhood retail corners are mostly caused by long-term changes in residential patterns and resulting market weakness, and the response of retailing to those changes. Governance problems, from taxation to services, relate back to changes in residential preferences and choices made in the housing market.

Complexities and changes in education, health, social service, law enforcement and the criminal justice system, transportation, job locations, and politics are all connected to changes in how people value various neighborhoods and the resulting residential location choices made in the metropolitan housing market.

Chapter Two describes the socioeconomic and policy forces that have, for several decades, reduced the relative value in the metropolitan marketplace of many city neighborhoods. Economic and social patterns, tendencies for those who are financially able to socioeconomically segregate themselves, transportation and development decisions, decisions to desegregate schools at the district level rather than housing at the metropolitan level, changes in industrial and retailing methods, have all been part of this devaluation. Given these forces, and the implicit societal housing policy that low income shelter will be provided by devaluing city neighborhoods, it was inevitable that some neighborhoods would lose a big chunk of both their intangible and tangible value.

However, this does not adequately explain why a particular central city neighborhood becomes the target of decline. Some initial weakness in the marketplace, in the value people give the place, has to begin the cycle of economic decline. It doesn't just happen randomly. Those who can, choose a new, stable, or revitalizing neighborhood. The declining neighborhood moves from those with more to those with fewer resources. Eventually the resources are no longer sufficient to maintain the physical conditions of this place. Difficult service conditions and expectations of inferior service results lead to a decline of public safety, education, and general neighborhood appearance. A cyclical self-feeding process has begun.

The initial marketplace weakness that occurs in some places and starts the cycle of decline has to do, in addition to the metropolitan and societal scale factors discussed earlier, with some combination of the following things. Inner city neighborhoods are older. Housing maintenance costs are often higher. Even where maintenance investment has been adequate, there is probably some marketplace obsolescence of the physical product of house and environs. Factors such as lot size, age, natural setting, house style, number of bathrooms, garages, open space, begin to be judged as not quite as good as more contemporary neighborhoods in that same geographic sector of the marketplace.

A neighborhood in a historically affluent or high-status sector of the metropolitan development pattern, it is less likely to undergo long-term and deep decline. Original neighborhood layout, proximity to amenities such as well-maintained open space, design and attractiveness, housing design and original construction quality make some places inherently more decline-resistant than others. If, as is often the case, these neighborhoods are also in a sector that has traditional status in the metropolitan market, they are even more resistant.

Neighborhoods with good original location and design are probably more able to successfully work through the stresses of racial integration. Racially integrated neighborhoods are very difficult to sustain. Research seems to show that black middle-income people prefer and will move into integrated neighborhoods, perhaps to be assured of continued high quality services. White people will remain in integrated neighborhoods, but as natural turnover occurs they will choose to move to non-integrated neighborhoods. The combination of these two movements will tend to transform places from integrated to predominantly black. Those neighborhoods that sustain long-term racial integration are aided by a basic physical attractiveness that makes people want to stay or move into a neighborhood and reduces their fear of change. Integration in these places is more likely to be racial, rather than racial and economic.

In general, the same attractiveness and design characteristics support stability of redeveloped areas. However, such areas may suffer from having been, in the first place, in a market sector with less status, and from design that was compromised in the interest of the economic "reality and practicality." Good original design, well-maintained, is vital to long-term economic viability.

If housing construction at the metropolitan fringe in the sector is desirable, moving quickly and able to continue with ample developable land, existing neighborhoods in the sector will more likely decline. If the neighborhood has a demographic profile showing large numbers of older people, turnover will accelerate. In the weak housing markets of the 1990s, creating a demand for replacement buyers in these neighborhoods will be critical and difficult.

If the inner neighborhoods of the geographic sector are viewed as troublesome and if their livability, human development qualities, and public service issues remain unsolved, nearby neighborhoods in that sector will be more subject to decline. If a real or perceived loss of quality of some service condition (especially public safety, education, and general neighborhood appearance and conditions) begins to occur in neighborhoods near troubled areas, the decline will spread. Or if fear of change judged to be negative begins to increase, with racial fears or perceptions, unfortunately, heading the list, the areas will be vulnerable to decline.

Some combination of the above leads to perceptions of what the marketplace is going to do to the place, and self-fulfilling prophecies of decline may lead to just that—an economically declining neighborhood. An economically declining neighborhood is one in which ownership or occupancy transfers tend to move properties from households with more to households with fewer resources, or where the incomes and resources of non-moving residents are declining. This has advantages for the larger society that wants to keep low income households in the city and doesn't want to pay taxes for low income housing assistance, as well as for some low income people to whom the shelter thereby becomes available. However, it is a threat to existing occupants and eventually threatens the entire city.

Owner occupancy begins to shift to rental. Rental housing need not be inferior housing, but the shift of single-family owner-occupied housing to renter-occupied housing is a problem or the indicator of a problem. The rental market may remain healthy for a time because people will become renters and live in areas where they might not choose to buy, and investors will become landlords where they would not be willing to live.

If the cycle continues, at some point the owners and occupants are unable to maintain or renew the structures. Deterioration follows. Self-fulfilling predictions about social conditions or investment risk feed the decline. Attempts by the public sector to fill the investment gap are usually relatively small compared to either the need or the magnitude of the private market competition, and are unable to catch up.

At some point in the process of decline, there is a disparity between what owners and occupants of low income private housing spend for property and shelter and what public policy would like them to spend. Because these owners and occupants either choose not to or cannot spend enough to maintain the housing's physical condition or to live elsewhere, government tries to increase spending by regulation, incentives, and investing public money. The inner city housing problem becomes one of too little private, and too much, but never enough, public investment.

Housing market research reveals why this is the case. Low income household expenditures have low housing elasticity, meaning that increased income is not spent on housing, but on other needs (Bourne, 130). This is not surprising, given proportions of income needed to meet minimum shelter and other needs. The public values housing expenditure more than low income households do.

Middle income households are more elastic in the housing market. Increases in income will generate more expenditure in housing, presumably because other needs have been met. Tax advantages and the increased income can be spent on the need or luxury of more housing. Thus we have the irony of increasing expenditure in new and high-priced housing, and decreasing expenditure in old and poor condition housing that needs more investment. Increased expenditure in higher income housing diverts savings and resources into consumption that would serve the national economy better if invested in capital plant and production, but national housing policy encourages the opposite. We end up with too much total investment in housing: too much private investment on the metropolitan fringe, not enough in the center; and too much, but not enough, public expenditure in the center.

The reverse situation, an economically revitalizing neighborhood, is one in which the market is on the upswing. Here transfers tend to move properties toward occupancy by those with more resources. Or you have a neighborhood in which the sustainable public intervention is greater than the investment gap between maintenance and renewal needs and available private expenditures.

Revitalization by regaining strength in the private market is usually viewed as positive by city government, bankers, realtors, and planners. But because declining neighborhoods account for most low income housing, this revitalization can work to the disadvantage of low income residents, present or future.

Intervention in the process of decline, or efforts to revitalize a neighborhood, need to be clear about just what is being attempted. If the intent is economic revitalization, that is increasing value in the marketplace, the supply of low income housing will be reduced. Unless that issue is addressed, revitalization will either not succeed or will push the unresolved need to some other place. Economic revitalization of neighborhoods as discussed in this paper should be carried out within the context of a strategy that addresses poverty, living conditions in areas more severely affected, low income housing supply and location, and transportation, development and job location patterns.

In Chapter Six, a process is discussed for improving the human development qualities in those neighborhoods that have more difficulties than those in which market revitalization can be the initial goal. Giving first emphasis to human conditions rather than the physical deficiencies of the place does not mean that some places will be written off for long-term economic and physical revitalization. It only means that where the initial conditions are thornier, the human development, livability, and public service conditions must be dealt with first. This is both because they are more important and because marketplace revitalization focusing only on physical and market conditions won't work anyway until service results and livability are improved.

In an oversimplified way, the thrust of this logic for the housing component of a revitalization program is that only where the house is "worse" than the neighborhood conditions will money spent on its removal or rehabilitation pay off in the marketplace. If the basic public conditions are continually improved, more and more housing will justify physical improvement beyond basic livability changes. Learning to adjust effort and expenditures between housing investment and general neighborhood investment, to maintain a steadily improving balance, is strategically essential.

Another way to make the same point is to assert that regardless of the long-range goal, the process, to succeed, needs to start at a place that fits the initial conditions, then proceed in a certain order. First, the basic conditions of livability and human development must be addressed. Second, the issues of how low income people are to be housed or achieve higher income must be considered and resolved. These two matters seem to be primarily the responsibility of or require a great deal of assistance from organizations larger than the neighborhood. One concern of neighborhood groups should be to push larger units to do these two things well to improve the success of neighborhood-scale work. Only then can marketplace revitalization proceed with some chance of success, without displacement of low income households to their disadvantage, and that of another neighborhood nearby, and with confidence that the higher goal of improving residents' well-being and life chances has been given priority.

The following discussion is intended to be about places where the first two issues have been dealt with or where conditions have not yet become difficult enough to require such emphasis. Places where intervention occurs earlier in the cycle of decline.

Marketplace Revitalization of Neighborhoods

Approaches to economic revitalization at the neighborhood level can be organized into a three-part strategy:

- Maintaining and upgrading the quality of the product
- Promoting and marketing the product
- Financing

Upgrading the Quality of the Housing and Neighborhood Product

When someone purchases or rents a housing unit they are getting not only shelter, but a whole bundle of goods and services (Adams; also Bourne, *The Geography of Housing*). This includes what the unit itself provides, such as shelter, comfort, privacy, investment, security, status, self-expression—a rather complex package for those who can buy more than just shelter. Beyond or in connection with the unit, the occupant gets access to a set of house services, utilities, police and fire protection, streets, transportation, public schools, parks, services provided by the government or service providers within which the unit stands.

The occupant gains proximity to jobs, commercial services, institutions, churches, a diverse set of possibilities, if useful or suitable choices exist in the vicinity of the housing unit. The occupant purchases the characteristics of the neighborhood: attractiveness and amenities, cleanliness, social status, security, perceived security of housing investment, diversity or homogeneity. Again, a varied package.

The point is that the housing product is a mix of things—much more than the house itself. It is, therefore, difficult to pinpoint just what the initial market weakness is that begins the decline of a neighborhood. Attempting to reverse that decline, that is, to reestablish the strength of the place in the private market, is considerably more complex than fixing houses. Deficiencies in the entire bundle of things that occupants buy must also be considered.

Market research has been done into what matters most in the housing product. Generally, research and common sense lead to the same conclusions. The private market insists on at least three necessary conditions beyond the house itself and the basic livability conditions discussed above and in Chapter Six: security, appearance and general condition, and access to a stable and functional educational system. Without these conditions, money spent on housing structures will not lead to sustained neighborhood revitalization.

The parallel here to maintaining high levels of human development and livability in the most difficult neighborhoods, discussed in Chapter Six, is a general philosophy of impeccable maintenance of public spaces, facilities, and rights of way. Also, available park and open space amenities are very important in the housing market and are a prime reason why large parts of Minneapolis are as attractive to the market as newer areas.

Beyond the questions of safety, attractiveness and education, and perhaps even more difficult to deal with, is the need to rebuild community. Certain social, cultural, and economic networks turn a place from mere shelter and space into a place that offers the feeling, sense and support of community, a place to belong. Neighborhoods of rapid turnover lose this and either decline or engage in revitalization that implies turnover of residents. The development of community is crucial to sustained revitalization, but we don't know enough about how it happens. A sense of the community value of a place is a protection against devaluation and decline that needs to be in place in successful community revitalization.

Removing large negatives, where possible, is part of improving product quality: reducing aircraft noise over parts of Minneapolis, adding strong open space features to match the power that lakes and parkways add to other areas, or reconciling land use conflicts.

In the 1990s, as the demographic demand decreases for the city's large supply of entry level housing, school issues will become increasingly important to central city competitiveness in the metropolitan housing market. Improving the image and product will be critical. Also, anything that softens the effect of the district boundary will help, whether properly designed choice programs, merged districts, shared facilities, or new metropolitan districts.

Survey research also shows that even if all these neighborhood factors are satisfactory in the marketplace, older housing often lacks such highly valued characteristics as extra bathrooms, two-car garages, and larger lots available with new housing. Programs to improve the existing housing product should research ways to add some of these elements to existing housing, and finance them.

If a combination of other programs is in place to improve the economic condition of low income households, as well as public assistance to improve their purchasing power in the private housing market, and to increase the supply of good quality and permanent low income housing throughout the regional market, it becomes arithmetically possible for revitalization to continue. If this is not the case, the revitalization of a neighborhood either will not be sustained, or another will decline to replace the low income housing function of the now too pricey revitalized place.

Promotion and Marketing of Housing and Neighborhood

Neighborhoods that are safe and clean, with good services and schools and modernized housing, don't always maintain or recover market soundness. Some things these places lack that new suburbs have are marketing offices, ads in the Sunday papers, pre-arranged financing packages—a whole set of features to make the new housing package as attractive and easy to purchase as possible. Given the real estate industry's uncertainty and ambivalence about central city living, older housing needs this marketing and promotion more than new housing.

Therefore, while the first priority is to improve the real quality of the housing and neighborhood product, another should be active promotion and marketing to maintain and restore perceptions. Cities have long been actively involved in the housing market, through renewal and rehabilitation programs and housing finance. Now they must get involved earlier in the process, closer to the initial causes of decline.

Successful maintenance and revitalization of city neighborhoods in the highly competitive markets of the 1990s will require action close to where the problem begins. The initial decline of a neighborhood starts with the day-to-day workings of the housing real estate market. Successful strategies need to perceive and intervene in these changes early, before the self-fulfilling prophecies of decline begin. Most public effort is late, when decline is well along.

If there is a sound reason for housing market value changes, then the issue is product quality, as discussed earlier. If not, the issue is one of improving perceptions and the image of the place, i.e., promotion and marketing. Image problems include not only a widely shared preference for suburban house and neighborhood styles, but also the broad negative perceptions of the "inner city" carried by a large segment of the population, and fed by day-to-day events, the media, and the real estate market itself. This may not be changeable in the short-range, or at all; it will be the context within which marketing strategies must work.

Private housing development is always accompanied by a marketing plan. The investment is somehow tied to market information, and a budget for promotion and marketing are simply part of the package. The most direct way to emulate this would be to create a public or private nonprofit real estate company, not managed by city government, that has, as its mission, the promotion and marketing of a neighborhood. It would do the market research, the promotion and advertising, the listing, the showing and selling components of an aggressive campaign to sustain a strong demand. Nonprofit or perhaps for-profit firms of this sort might be city-wide or by community. They would be intended to balance any inaccurate downplaying of city housing in the real estate industry, as well as provide the level of promotion and assistance to potential buyers that new housing offers.

There are perhaps objections to this idea that have to do with private versus public enterprise, potential displacement of already existing private firms, and lack of access to information shared by real estate multiple listing groups. Whether or not city or neighborhood real estate firms can or should be put in place, the idea illustrates the importance of marketing and promotion in sustaining city neighborhoods.

Perhaps less threatening would be a neighborhood management process in which someone employed by a neighborhood organization has full-time responsibility for seeing and resolving

issues of quality and marketing. If this role were performed by a
realtor, and the management role also earned some competitive
advantage in listing and marketing neighborhood housing, the cost
to residents of such a management, ombudsman, and marketing
service might be affordable.

Short of these organizational approaches, a neighborhood
needs to have a marketing and promotion program. This needs to
reflect the real conditions, and emphasize the positive themes of the
city generally and the specific amenities of the particular neighborhood.

Ample, Readily Available, and Favorable Financing for City Neighborhood Housing

To the buyer of a new suburban house, qualifying for and arranging
financing is almost an incidental part of the process. A relationship
between the developer and financial institution(s) is already in
place; the financing is reserved, terms and mortgage agreed upon,
and perhaps an advantageous rate offered to the developer in order
to get the financing business. The institution already knows the
specific product, the unblemished though unfinished neighborhood,
and the characteristics of the entire smaller municipality. The
developer is the advocate and red tape cutter for the other half of
the equation—the buyer. Also, the buyer probably has fewer characteristics that might cause the financier to hesitate.

Neighborhood revitalization efforts need to more nearly repli-
cate the financing situation of new housing. City and state programs
have improved the availability and favorability of financing for
existing and city housing, but have probably complicated rather
than simplified the process. The existing maze of state and city
programs may need to be replaced with the concept of tiering (see
Figure 9), from city-wide to neighborhood to individual house to
buyer need.

In the simplest city-wide feature of a tiered system, all buyers
of homes in which the purchase will not change the tenure status
would be offered financing at an interest rate (perhaps 1 percent)
below the metropolitan market rate. This would be contingent upon
the unit not moving from owner to rental status for purchase or
rehabilitation work, perhaps to repair code problems found in a
"truth in housing" inspection at time of sale. This would not be tied
to income or neighborhood, but would simply become a new,
simple, and widely-known fact in the metropolitan housing market.
Anyone can buy anywhere in the central city and their mortgage
interest rate will be less. Buy elsewhere or leave the city and it will
be more. Period.

The purpose is not redistributional or neighborhood specific,
but to counteract the general societal bad rap of central city living.

If a universal mortgage assistance does not seem directed at what we want, it could perhaps be a rehabilitation incentive. Simple universality for anyone anywhere in the city, so that everybody in the metropolitan market process knows about it, is the key point.

Further, in certain neighborhoods where early market weakness has been detected, additional incentives should be available to anyone anywhere in that neighborhood. This could be a yet more favorable interest rate, or low-priced renovation financing, or a renovation grant. Again, it should not be tied to income because the goal is not to reduce the income profile of the neighborhood, but to strengthen a neighborhood in the metropolitan marketplace before self-fulfilling prophecies of decline begin, and serious investment gaps begin to feed the downward spiral.

This selective stacking of benefits could be extended to individual houses in a critical neighborhood or occasional critical houses in good neighborhoods. The point would be to lure private capital into difficult situations to overcome market weakness. If in each case the incentive were 1 percent, someone who renovated a strategically needy house in a tippy neighborhood in Minneapolis would have a total incentive of 3 percent.

Using interest rates as the carrot has some disadvantages. The full impact is not obtained because of interest rate income tax deductibility. But assisting with purchases does result in stronger neighborhoods. A possible advantage is that a fixed interest rate subsidy is proportionally more important when interest rates are low. Given that this tends to happen during recessions, it might have a built-in counter-recession effect for the city's housing.

This requires, as any effective revitalization program must, a distinction between shelter programs for those in severe need, and efforts to physically and economically revitalize a neighborhood— the two being quite different things.

Whether a house needs rehabilitation or a family needs shelter assistance are two different issues. They should not automatically be worked together. We tend to lump them together because of the unwillingness to recognize the different objectives of shelter and revitalization: for a source of funds for physical projects and because low income families can be used (misused) to fill in areas the normal market has rejected. Neither social nor revitalization goals are really advanced by this practice. The two needs should be separated.

All programs should be recast into either, but not both, of two objectives: funding for shelter assistance for low income people and physical and marketplace revitalization of housing and neighborhoods. Program crossover between these objectives should occur where and if both shelter assistance and revitalization are adopted policy goals for the neighborhood and project, and if other conditions necessary for successful revitalization have been met.

Shelter assistance benefits for low income households might or might not be used in conjunction with and accumulated with city-wide, neighborhood and housing programs. It is not, however, appropriate to depend upon shelter benefits as the core financing for neighborhood revitalization. The purposes are different, funds get diverted from shelter to structural purposes, and dependence upon the needy as a source of financing for projects will not lead to long-run economic revitalization of a city's neighborhoods.

Figure 9 is intended to make two points. First, that shelter assistance and physical revitalization objectives and financing programs must and can be separated. Second, that in so doing, financing systems can be put in place that are more powerful than the present mess in the marketplace.

This may not be the right approach, but something like it needs to be considered. The present hodgepodge of overlapping housing finance programs obscures even from practitioners the original purposes of each, and no one knows the cumulative impact. More importantly, the potential marketplace and promotional incentive of a more direct and clear program is lost, and with it potential leverage and linkage into the private market, where most housing improvement money will have to come from.

Conclusions

In the long run, city neighborhoods would benefit from a shift in the negative marketplace and societal view of central and inner city conditions. Without this shift there will be a constant impulse toward underinvestment and abandonment of inner city housing. While it is difficult to be optimistic that these changes will occur soon, very large increases in transportation costs, environmental crises, political leadership, and improved regional and national housing policy might eventually accomplish such a shift.

In the meantime, stabilization and revitalization of most city neighborhoods should consist of vigorous programs to improve the central city house and neighborhood product. Prevailing attitudes in the metropolitan housing marketplace must be overcome with programs to promote and market that housing and neighborhood product aggressively, with extensive use of financing as an equalizer.

Figure 9. Concept of Rationalized Housing Finance System

To revitalize neighborhoods, use
> **mortgage interest rate incentives:**

Citywide "perception" incentives	1%
Selected neighborhood "reinvestment" incentives	1%
Substandard house "rehabilitation" incentives	1%
Maximum package of combined revitalization incentives	3%

To shelter low income people, use
> **need-based sliding scale shelter assistance:**

Low need	$
Medium need	$$
High need	$$$
Maximum shelter assistance	$$$

Maximum, if combined, revitalization incentives
and shelter assistance: 3% + $$$

Chapter Eight

The Metropolitan Development, Job, Housing and Transportation Component of an Inner City Revitalization Strategy

A metropolis is something more than a small city
grown large, with other cities clustered about it. For
in the process of its growth, it acquires new needs,
new methods, a new viewpoint.

Austin F. Macdonald, 1929,
p. 122.

Anthony Downs has recently described the national metropolitan
development dilemma in a way that accurately portrays the situation in Minneapolis-St. Paul and most other medium-sized and
larger metropolitan areas. Downs describes the metropolitan
development vision throughout the United States as one of universal ownership of a single-family home in a small, self-governing
community distant from the workplace; universal car ownership; a
workplace in a low-rise, park-like setting with immediately
adjacent parking. Not a bad vision, but Downs points out some
flaws (*City Planning and Management News*, September, 1989,
"The Need for a New Vision Of Our Urban Future," excerpted
from National Press Club Speech, May 31, 1989).

The envisioned low density development and separated work
and residences means massive movement of automobiles and resultant air pollution, energy addiction, and traffic congestion. Downs
points out that while traffic congestion occurs near high density
development, it is caused by auto-dependent low density development and separated land uses. The next flaw is that the vision only
provides well for high-cost housing that only a fraction of the
population can afford.

Finally, the vision doesn't provide for governmental ability to cut through its own fragmentation and solve the environmental, housing and other problems at the necessary metropolitan scale. Given these flaws, the results don't match the vision. Elaborating on the flaws, Downs notes, must include the expectation that poor people are to have no discernible presence in this development vision. The same is true of people of color, unless they are few and very clearly middle class or wealthy. The underlying assumption of almost everyone involved in planning, implementing, financing, governing and living in that development vision is that low income people and most minorities are to be housed somewhere else, by the inevitable devaluation of central city neighborhoods.

The vision very much values homogeneity of income, status, and skin color. This desire for homogeneity is a major driver of the vision and is thus a cause in the waste of the environment, of existing development, of energy and other resources, of capital required for its maintenance. In addition to requiring the concentration of low income and minorities in the inner city, it also assumes and requires under-investment, deterioration, and some abandonment of the inner city.

Another flaw in this vision is that productive use of land is considered inferior to consumptive and dead-end land use. The existing resource of developed urban land is rejected. Agriculture is considered a non-use; industry is only for tax base; office space is considered better; retail even better; and high value residential, an almost entirely consumptive use of land, is most favored of all. The less productive the use, the more it is valued in this vision.

In this vision, moving land from production (agriculture) to consumption (residential) is called "development." Yet in any but the most short-sighted and narrow sense of the term development, this shift of land use and resources is just the opposite—a reduction rather than an increase in long-term aggregate productive and economic potential.

There is in this vision little provision for future generations' need for productive land, resources and natural environment. Growth now, even in the face of ample and perhaps surplus housing, retail space, and office space is valued over environmental and other future resource conservation, or any other concern for the future. The vision is indeed flawed, as Down suggests, and its long-term results will be a millstone around the neck of the national economy whenever the global Rube Goldberg petroleum machine malfunctions, and as environmental predictions approach reality.

Downs recommends a new vision to include the following ideas:

- Large areas of moderately high-density development of both housing and workplaces to reduce travel needs.

- Development that is a blend of housing styles, prices and types near jobs.
- Adequate state government-legislated area-wide planning processes and institutions, but not abandonment of local sovereignty.
- No dependence upon rail mass transit if federal subsidies are required, because that means it won't happen.
- High-density suburban workplaces redesigned more like downtowns with pedestrian movement among complexes possible.
- Some low income households, accessible to the new job locations.

It is fortuitous that essentially the same remedies are needed to correct both the social and environmental malfunctioning of the present development vision. The improvements suggested by Downs would help both. If his and some other ideas could be incorporated into metropolitan-scale development policy and practice, it may be possible to avoid backtracking on social advancement as our attention turns to environmental and other realities of the 1990s.

During the next decade or so, environmental reality will cause a fundamental shift in attitudes about development and economic growth. The answer to "How much economic growth do we want?" will no longer be "As much as we can get!" The era of "Yes, but" economic imperialism will end. "Yes, but doing that would hurt economic growth" will no longer be an automatic stifler of environmental, conservation and social justice proposals. "Yes, but doing that will damage the environment" may replace it.

We will then be forced at the national and metropolitan scale to decide how much and what kind of economic growth we really need to be a thriving society. If we are farsighted and lucky, national economic policy will recognize the crucial role of successful metropolitan development as a cornerstone of successful national development. This may force the needed metropolitan scale responses.

Answers to difficult economic questions that only consider how big and fast the economy is producing and consuming (i.e., Gross National Product, car and housing production, gross employment, money flows) will not enlighten or resolve either social or environmental problems. Such answers will promote economic development in only superficial and short-sighted ways.

There will be a strong tendency for economic growth constrained by real environmental risk to most deeply affect low income, unprepared households and add considerably to inner city problems if the conventional indicators of economic growth are drivers of economic policy. The indicators that should be heeded concern aggregate accumulation and distribution of wealth and goods within the economy and society. Emphasis upon these kinds of indicators should replace or override the present myopic and misleading preoccupation with rate of consumption as the key indicator of economic strength. This shift of emphasis from today's sacred economic indicators would reveal that real economic strength, environmental protection, and social well-being of all people are not conflicting aspirations that must be either dominated by economic thought or, at best, balanced. In the long run they are all the same thing.

More relevant indicators would reveal that a high-quality useful product that lasts for a long time and accumulates in society continues to add as much to real economic wealth as does the current year's new production. It is also less environmentally degrading and resource wasteful. Proper indicators would reveal very few shortages of anything important. The mind set of our being a shortage economy that must race to produce more in order to survive is as antiquated as the economic teachings that perpetuate it.

Proper indicators would eliminate or soften the myth that private activity is always economic growth and public activity is never economic growth. An innovative public school building that provides a successful setting for present and future education, public or private health programs for children; spending money to maintain public safety and education standards in low income neighborhoods so people can lead and prepare for successful lives— these activities add real assets and economic strength. The addition of a fourth bathroom to an oversized, under-occupied house, or the purchase of a Jaguar automobile by a household or a business add little more than increased overhead cost. Some public sector production and consumption adds to real economic strength; some does not. The same is true of private sector consumption and production. Present indicators don't capture this. They mislead economic and tax policy.

This discussion is not intended as an argument for central planning of the private economic sector. It argues that an affluent society that feels it can't afford public sector actions that strengthen the community, society and economy, but spends freely on noneconomy building private consumption, represents the victory of short-sighted rhetorical dogmatism over common sense.

Why does a metropolitan area, city or state need economic development and growth? Even conservative politicians fall back on jobs as their most popular indicator of and justification for economic growth. When they do this they are admitting that a crucial and perhaps primary function of the economy in an affluent society is to do what jobs do: distribute income and thereby serve as an acceptable and efficient method for distribution of goods, services and wealth. Obviously, producing goods, services and wealth is necessary or there would be nothing to distribute. However, present indicators pay almost no attention to the distributional qualities of the economy and therefore don't illuminate job needs or policies well. The distributional characteristics of national and metropolitan economies and economic policy should be given a great deal more attention.

The connection of this line of thought to poverty and inner city conditions is as follows. There is clearly a societal consensus that most poverty reduction will occur through work-derived income rather than governmental transfer payments. Therefore, a shortage or maldistribution of meaningful and remunerative work *guarantees* that poverty and inner city conditions will continue and get worse. This tells us that economic development policy will need to be centered on the redistribution of work and work opportunity if it is to address inner city issues.

A new type of economic indicator will reveal that we are not a shortage economy as such, but that even in an affluent economy there can be a real shortage of meaningful work that pays enough to adequately redistribute well-being. Failure to achieve this adequate distribution is close to the root causes of poverty and inner city conditions.

This line of thought connects in several places to metropolitan-scale planning and policy. Metropolitan economies are more real and less artificially bounded than city, state and perhaps even national economies. A successful national economy will, in the next decade and century, increasingly become the sum of metropolitan economies that perform well in the "new global economy." Meaningful analysis and planning for economic success can take place at the metropolitan scale. Metropolitan areas that want to reestablish themselves as national leaders in metropolitan planning have a real chance to demonstrate innovative economic indicators; to do some creative and groundbreaking analysis; and to pilot new kinds of synergistic rather than competing or "balanced" social, environmental and economic policy and programs. This could be done at the metropolitan scale much better than it can or will be done at the city, state or national scale.

We need a new wave of metropolitan planning. The major objectives should be to prepare for the new environmental reality, to look at economic development from a somewhat different viewpoint, and to improve inner city and social conditions. These are the most important development issues facing most metropolitan areas, including the Twin Cities.

That new round of planning should begin with a discussion of how much and what kind of growth we need to provide the jobs needed to distribute economic well-being in a socially responsible way, while being environmentally farsighted.

The discussion needs to redefine the meaning of "development." The new definition needs to have something to do with public and private investment that adds to the net economic, natural, social, cultural and human capital and strength of the metropolitan area. The old definition that often means the shift of land from production to consumption uses, from natural to man-made functions, that results in overall increase in public and private costs, and a net loss of strength, should be discarded and that practice renamed.

The next discussion should be about the extent of urbanization needed for this growth. That discussion will, in all probability, reveal that there is absolutely no need now or in the future to extend urban scale services and development beyond present boundaries and that these should be considered fixed, or even reduced. The argument that this will increase the cost of new housing is false.

The more the urbanized portion of the region spreads out, the greater the isolation of inner city neighborhoods and households from job and other opportunity growth. And the more vulnerable the entire metropolitan area will be to the emerging energy, air quality and other environmental realities of the 1990s.

This will require state government to begin doing state planning, including statewide development and land use planning. It should also lead to state development policy that essentially halts the conversion of land from sensitive natural or productive uses to consumption uses and focuses all new land conversion within existing towns, growth centers and recreation areas.

This planning should consider the possibility that diversity is a form of economic strength and that the entire state might be better off if the metropolitan areas grew less and more support were given to maintaining strong communities outstate. Or it might lead to strategies for using metropolitan areas as economic development magnets in the new high-tech and service-oriented global economy. Or deliberate programs to spin off some of that metropolitan good fortune to outstate communities in the form of industrial development, jobs or other benefits. In these or others ways it should definitely attempt to mend the outstate/metropolitan splintering that serves as a convenient, but over-simplified and debilitating political issue. State-scale development planning should lead to more use of state resources, and of the human service-oriented state administrative structure, in solving difficult inner city issues.

Within the context created by this overall growth discussion, by tightening urban growth boundaries, by new state development policy and by the metropolitan choice in housing strategy covered in Chapter Eight, more optimistic metropolitan-scale planning for improved patterns and connection of jobs, housing and transportation can take place. The underlying goals should be reduction of poverty; reconnection of inner city neighborhoods and households to the larger economy and opportunity; long-term elimination of inner city conditions; and mutually supportive social, economic and environmental development.

During the 1980s other states and metropolitan areas have developed and legislated development management and planning that is more effective than that now in place in Minnesota and the Twin Cities. As Downs says, the Oregon model is probably the best. Florida, New Jersey, Georgia, Maine, Rhode Island, Vermont and Massachusetts all have enacted state, regional, and local development legislation since the Twin Cities system was conceived in the 1970s. This legislation generally deals with environment, facilities, development, and requirements for provision of suburban low income housing that could help inner city problems. However, these were not developed as strategies deliberately focused on inner city problems, nor does there seem to be such a focused regional strategy in place anywhere.

The Oregon method has worked the best of any in the country for several reasons. First, the legislation establishing the Portland process was statewide and put in place statewide planning goals that had to be achieved in local plans. The legislation doesn't just set up a planning process, it includes some substantive goals and requires results. Second, there are relatively few local government units in the Portland metropolitan area. This makes metropolitan planning simpler and reduces the size of the political army of local government participants threatened by effective metropolitan action. Third, in addition to environmental and other goals, the state goals require all local governments to develop a full range of price and density housing within their boundaries, irrespective of the availability of federal funding for that housing. Fourth, the non-profit group, 1,000 Friends of Oregon, serves as a tough watchdog to see that the spirit and content of planning and development legislation is not negotiated away by or among governmental units. Through observation, lobbying, legislative proposals, and court challenges they play a much more forceful role than any such organization in Minnesota.

Some factors in the success of the Portland model are transferable; others, such as the number of local governmental units, are less so. In any case, in Oregon and other states a contemporary set of ideas is available. These ideas need to be examined for usefulness and transferability in enabling legislation to set the stage for creative metropolitan-scale planning.

Techniques

The elaborate metropolitan transportation and development simulation models developed by the Metropolitan Council and other agencies should be subject to a different type of scrutiny.

The travel data should be used to examine the degree of isolation of low income areas by comparing travel patterns with those of more "average" areas.

The models should be used to reveal and define the obvious areas of low income housing, low income, and high unemployment. These should become the highest priority metropolitan job development areas, with special transportation attention, financial support and other metropolitan-scale programs.

Areas of high employment growth should also be defined and given highest priority for development of large amounts of low income housing and associated services. Major employment growth beyond the I-694/494 beltway should be prevented.

The transportation system should be examined for weak links between jobs, low income housing, and the highest priority for service and facilities should go to improving these links. Light rail transit planning should be focused on this opportunity.

The basic purpose of the light rail system proposal should be reconsidered. The present "path of least resistance" planning and political philosophy in light rail development will not serve any purpose very well. If the system were really intended to reduce congestion and energy consumption and convert automobile riders to transit riders, it must be an express system with few stops. While this would have the same weakening effect as the freeway system upon the central city housing market, it would perform some useful purpose. On the other hand, the system could be designed to bolster the development strength and livability of the inner part of the metropolitan region. The intent would be to create an area where people could live, work, and build an urban life style around high quality transit, rather than owning one or more automobiles.

Such a system would initially be limited to the central cities; a few suburbs; and the interconnecting of the downtowns, cultural and educational facilities, high-density housing and job clusters. It would not expect to significantly reduce automobile traffic in the short run, but to lay the groundwork for a long-term, less auto-dependent development pattern. This approach strengthens and diversifies that part of the city within which most low income families live, improves their transportation options, helps reconnect the inner city to the larger region, and could be the basis for reverse commuting from inner city residential areas to suburban job clusters.

In either case, the fundamental planning equation must be tight interconnecting of development, job location, low income housing, and transportation. Proposals to extend light rail transit and urban transit to distant places should be set aside unless very effective state development regulations are in place. In the absence of such regulation, a sprawling transit system will feed an economically, financially, environmentally, and socially unsound development pattern and increase energy consumption rather than reduce it. It will continue the fragmentation of metropolitan areas in ways similar to the freeway system.

Transit illustrates the several steps in successful implementation of improved metropolitan development patterns. Development regulation is needed, but alone it isn't enough. Diminishing the marketplace power of sprawling development requires that a better pattern be made highly attractive in the marketplace. This requires multiple approaches somewhat similar to strengthening the marketability of central city neighborhoods as discussed in Chapter Seven. Most of all, some expectation of better results, a higher vision of what is possible, some statements of clear unambiguous public interest, should become part of development discussion and policy.

Simply accepting the segregationist housing market dynamics, the environmental damage, and the economic and social millstones of the "development process" as free market inevitability is not appropriate in something so publicly subsidized, so dependent upon public infrastructure spending and with so many other long-term public ramifications. An improved development vision is needed.

The relative marketability of existing, close-in and fill-in development can be improved in several ways. First, any local government unit that develops or is developed should have a state-mandated responsibility to permit and provide significant amounts of low income and higher-density housing within its boundaries, particularly if there is proximate existing or planned job growth or urban transit. The escape route from the central city or first ring suburbs to white, affluent, low-density communities should be severed by removing any right of a governmental unit to so segregate itself through public policy. The difference in the marketplace among older, existing, and new development would be thereby reduced, as would the separationist dynamics of the metropolitan housing market.

A graduated or stepped system of development fees, as is being considered in Florida, should be examined. In this system, fringe areas would pay very high development fees to cover all local and metropolitan public costs of each new housing unit. Within the partially developed areas the fees would be less. In certain inner city or older suburban areas there would be no fee. There might even be financial incentives. A variation of this is the idea of luxury taxes on higher-priced and newer construction in order to encourage a shift of resources from new to existing and from consumption to more productive investment, with the revenues used to finance publicly assisted housing or to underwrite inner city redevelopment costs.

The metropolitan land to be developed at urban density and provided with urban public services should, as in the Twin Cities, Portland and a few other places, be clearly and firmly delineated and bounded. There should be little expectation that it will ever be enlarged. Outside of these areas, conversion of land from productive uses and land parcelization should cease. Large park reserves and greenbelts of public or development restricted land might, eventually, permanently bound or contain primary areas of urban densities and services. Someone should then calculate the amount of tree growth that would be required to replace the carbon dioxide taken out of the atmosphere by the contained urban process and try to design a green belt large enough to provide it. In the event the need for urban land is underestimated, portions of these reserves could be released, with the public as the beneficiary of interim land price inflation. The market attractiveness of the developed area can be further enhanced by services quality and special services, by the placement of public and institutional facilities, and by careful metropolitan-scale public policy involvement in the location of job producing development.

Finally, the ability of closer-in areas to attract market and investment depends upon high quality design that either achieves in a higher density urban setting the pleasantness that households seek on the semi-pristine development fringe, or shows them something even more attractive in the form of exciting urbanity.

While part of an improved development vision can be implemented through regulation, long-term success requires showing people a better product. Closer-in areas already have location advantages that will become increasingly important in the environmentally driven future. That location advantage can be packaged with financial incentives, sharing of social responsibility, quality services, facilities, and a lot of attention to exciting, attractive, human-oriented design to get that better product.

Conclusions

Among public policy people, there is a prevailing sense that in places that were leaders in metropolitan organization and planning, most metropolitan-scale challenges and issues have been met and resolved. This is inaccurate. Responses to the most important metropolitan challenges have hardly begun. In the 1990s, metropolitan policy making will need to replace current growth-dominant views of economic development with new mutually supportive environmental, social and economic development visions. A major goal of this vision must be to reduce poverty and eliminate concentrations of people and place-destroying inner city conditions. These conditions are fundamentally a result of how the metropolitan development process aggravates and concentrates societal poverty. Lasting improvement requires effective metropolitan approaches and organizations.

Metropolitan-scale economic analysis could develop more innovative and meaningful ways of measuring economic development than those now dominant. These could, in turn, lead to mutually supportive and synergistic rather than competitive or "balanced" social, environmental, and economic growth goals and programs. This sort of development planning in an affluent society within an environmentally damaged world will need to pay more attention to the distributive powers of the economy. This will reduce the low income and poverty causes of inner city problems while emphasizing environmental and resource conservation.

Metropolitan planning for development, jobs, housing, and transportation arrangements within a deliberately constrained urban development area can simultaneously address and improve social and environmental situations and provide an economically less burdensome development pattern. This is the challenge for a badly needed new wave of metropolitan planning.

Through design, financial incentives, services, facilities and regulation the present ailing and destructive vision of metropolitan development can be replaced with a new, more effective, more environmentally sound, more humane, more just, and more economically sound development vision.

The next and final chapter will propose neighborhood, city and metropolitan leadership and partnerships at their levels of origin and solution.

Chapter Nine

Building Leadership, Partnerships and Organization for a Unified Metropolitan Inner City Strategy

Error is most difficult to correct when it has become
a way of life.

Aaron Wildavsky, 1987, p. 399.

The previous chapters have asserted that the concentration of poverty, and associated social, economic and physical conditions in the
inner city is the problem most threatening to the livability, governance and economic well-being of central cities. It is also the most
important metropolitan development issue.

The causes of this inner city situation are poverty, housing
market dynamics and policy that concentrate that poverty into the
inner city, a wide range of private and public actions that further
isolate the inner city, and service failures that deepen the problem.
Eventually, some places become not only the recipients of poverty
and low income households, but causes of further poverty.

Intervention in this situation requires a multifaceted and multilevel strategy. Work to be done comes under these headings:

* poverty reduction;

* improving the livability and human development characteristics of low income neighborhoods;

* intervention in the regional housing market;

* increasing the housing market strength of central city neighborhoods; and

* improving metropolitan-scale development, housing, job
  location and transportation planning.

This chapter considers ways of developing a metropolitan
sense of responsibility and mission for:

* improving inner city conditions;

- reducing the dissociation of the metropolitan society from inner city and poverty situations;

- reaching consensus about a strategy for better distributed responsibility for implementing various strategy components; and

- building the leadership and partnerships needed for success.

Leadership makes a difference, makes things come out better. Power alone only makes things come out different for the sake of ego and self-interest; leadership is a selective use of power. The leadership that is needed to address the topics of this report will change and improve our urban society, economies, housing markets, development patterns, public policy-making about poverty and the inner city.

In his teaching and writing, Dr. Robert Terry of the Reflective Leadership Center, Hubert H. Humphrey Institute of Public Affairs, University of Minnesota, tells us that leadership is about ethical missions and the application of power, structure, and resources toward those missions. In his *Human Action Diagnostic Tool*, Dr. Terry arranges mission, power, structure and resources vertically within a context of movement from present existence toward meaning that gives significance to human action. Dr. Terry often uses this vertical arrangement to make the point that whatever we think the issue is, it is really the next level above or higher and we typically and mistakenly try to deal with it at the next level below or lower.

For example, when we set out to solve inner city issues, the typical first response is "give us more resources," when the fundamental problems and previous "solutions" really go back to distribution of power, market and governmental organization and structure, not to mention muddy or inaccurate missions. While more resources are part of the solution, they won't achieve permanent improvement unless something else changes. Fixing houses with public money won't achieve permanent neighborhood improvement when the metropolitan housing market is sucking out resources faster than the public sector can replace them. We need to look at the power, structure and mission of the metropolitan housing market and housing policy. If we don't want or are unable to change these factors, our neighborhoods will continue to deteriorate, no matter how much money we funnel into them.

Or we may wish to change the mission to one of achieving successful low income neighborhoods where people can live or prepare to live successful lives. Then we would assign the mission to, or create, or give the power to, a structure that deals with safety, health, education, and other conditions for successful lives. We would not follow the usual pattern of automatically assigning the problem to a housing agency and seeking more housing resources.

A good, creative example of this kind of thinking is community policing. This response to neighborhood problems permits relooking at mission, realigning power, new organizational structures. It does not assume that more resources is the sole solution.

Mission

The six strategy elements discussed in earlier chapters represent an attempt to define or redefine purpose and mission vis-a-vis inner city conditions and solutions. Others may see the components differently. The important point here is that the mission should not be assumed to be obvious, understood and accepted. In something as complex as inner city issues, there is rarely a clear consensus about whether or to what degree the underlying mission focuses on people, physical conditions, or economics.

This report presents the mission as, first of all, concerned with people and how well their lives go. If that is the case, it would require a serious redefinition of mission and purpose to achieve both consensus and a sense of responsibility for the problems and solutions.

There seem to be three possible ways to get people to want to do public things, to assume some responsibility for situations larger than themselves: logic, idealism and fear (enlightened self-interest). For example, this report has tried to build a logical cause-and-effect argument that metropolitan-scale markets, development processes, social patterns and public actions cause inner city conditions. Therefore, metropolitan-scale solutions are needed and metropolitan-wide sharing of responsibility for improvement is appropriate.

A more idealistic argument is that poverty and racism are the root causes of inner city conditions and both these causes and the result are inconsistent with the ideals of democracy and capitalism, with the teachings of religion, with the voice of conscience. We should do better than this because our ideals are higher than this. This is not the "pursuit of happiness" our founding fathers had in mind.

The enlightened self-interest, or fear as intense self-interest, or the "Henny Penny, the sky is falling" approach is the one most used in planning and public policy discussion. If you don't do something about the causes of inner city conditions, the situation will spread and those people will come to your neighborhood or your downtown and commit crimes, or even move in.

If we don't solve race, education, poverty and employment issues, who will be paying into the unfunded and demographically shaky Social Security system in the next century? What happens to your retirement security if next century's non-white majority becomes unwilling to make the larger employee and employer payments that changing ratios of workers to retirees will require?

Of course logic, idealism and fear are drivers of inertia as well as change. Keep these people in the inner city and we will move away from them and create a new local government and community situation that discourages or prevents their following. This has elements of logic, idealism, fear and enlightened self-interest. There are fascinating paradoxes here.

If people, individually, could indeed control who lives next door, maybe they wouldn't create entire communities to achieve the same end. Since such individual selection is a logical and constitutional impossibility, more elaborate and subtle mechanisms— housing policy and markets, governmental structure, and economic patterns—are used to achieve similar, more aggregated results. The result is not only the aggregation that is the sought-after community, but also the aggregate undesirable result—inner city conditions, that are larger, more concentrated, more isolated, more debilitating to those caught in them, and more costly and perhaps dangerous to the rest of society.

We are, of course, meddling in rather basic human characteristics, natural tendencies, "free" markets, and other "unchangeable," even sacred stuff. However, if the only purpose of government and social organization were to help people carry out all their "natural" tendencies, anarchy or perhaps theocracy would seem to do as well as any other form of governance. Not all natural characteristics of governments, markets, or individuals are noble.

Logic and understanding of cause and effect tell us that even our most revered natural, social and economic systems can act in unforeseeable and uncomfortable ways. Idealism, higher principles, constitutions are intended to achieve higher, more noble "natural" ends. Experience, fear, and enlightened self-interest have long since caused everyone to abandon the idea of a totally unmanaged society and economy.

No one really believes that passive, non-intervening reactivity is the way to better individual lives, better communities, a better country. We all believe that at some level our individual or collective acting on events will make things better. In public policy discussion, differences are not about passivity, but about desired outcomes, appropriate means and how fundamental the change we should or can hope to achieve. There is clearly a public mission to do something about inner city conditions and the racial and poverty issues that lie behind them. Something needs to be done that spans the neighborhood, city, metropolitan and social components. It requires looking at the distribution of power.

Power

Governmental power in the United States resides basically with a granting of power to a federal system, from individuals as citizens, voters and constituents. This power is allocated via the national constitution to the executive, legislative and judicial branches of the federal government and, perhaps more importantly in this discussion, to state governments. State government may, at its discretion, allocate or reallocate power to cities, towns, counties and other forms of local government through constitutions, charter and legislation.

If reallocation of local and metropolitan governmental power were necessary to achieve an inner city improvement strategy, it would require actions of state government. The existing power arrangement is not sacred, but is the cumulative result of a multitude of decisions designed to respond to needs as they evolved. If needs are now seen differently, further change is entirely appropriate. Governmental units are not in place to serve themselves, political or bureaucratic systems or tradition, but to serve the citizenry that granted the power in the first place.

The power that drives the creation of inner city conditions is, of course, not just public, but, to a considerable degree, private. It takes the form of the metropolitan housing market, individual preferences, all sorts of institutions, financing patterns that together concentrate and isolate the inner city.

To say this is private power is not to say it is, or approaches being, a free market. It is heavily driven and underwritten by housing subsidies, public infrastructure investment, local government and other regulation and tax policy. Intervention to get different results is not intervening in a free market. There is certainly doubt about whether we know how to intervene for better results, but not about whether the public should intervene in the housing market. We already do. The question is whether we can change present intervention and power arrangements, not whether we are meddling in a free market.

Chapter Five advocates putting more power into the hands of low income households by providing ample choices for their housing location throughout the metropolitan area, and thus more nearly emulating private market conditions. This would mean that low income households would select the package of location, school districts, neighbors, proximity to jobs, neighborhood amenities— institutions that market rate buyers have. Just as the marketplace, through this selection process, optimizes the value of private expenditures, such a choice in low income housing would lead to better value from public housing assistance dollars. If effective, self-sufficiency training programs are successfully tied to housing assistance, the long-range mission becomes a creation of economic power in present low income households and an increase in the aggregate power of the entire community and economy.

Other ideas in this report have also to do with the power of individuals, low income households, and neighborhoods. Chapter Six considers neighborhood and community power. John McKnight suggests emphasizing the capabilities of individuals and neighborhoods rather than weaknesses, shifting power from bureaucracy to neighborhoods to enable them to develop their own agendas. He believes that this will have a synergistic, power-creating effect. It would further require existing governmental organizations to either step aside or take direction from neighborhood agendas. This is a proposal for major power shifting.

In the heat of neighborhood and community activism, the power shift usually called for and applauded is from the bureaucracy to the people. What is meant is a shift from the bureaucracy to a neighborhood organization that may or may not represent "the people," that is, have a legitimate grant of power from individuals in the community. Effective and legitimate neighborhood organizations for revitalization require consolidation of power from both directions—from individuals and property owners on the one hand and from larger organizations on the other.

Strategic community organizing requires gaining power from both individuals and larger organizations—using the power wrested from larger organizations to persuade individuals to participate in and further empower a movement. This process uses power to leverage more power. This is not easy. Stable or growing organizations are deemed necessary for rewards, security, status, and career advancement by individuals in both public and private bureaucracies. Power rearrangements threaten the structure and resources that provide this. Further, some believe in the correctness of the missions and means now in place. However, present power arrangements come from legislation and traditions, not from a divinity, and can legitimately be changed if change is necessary to accomplish a well-defined, thoughtful and useful mission. The common practice of changing power and organization without knowing why, but in hope that things will somehow get better is, however, not so legitimate.

Implementing the ideas in this report would require some redistribution of existing and creation of new power. The shifts would tend to be toward lower income people, away from the metropolitan housing market as it now operates, toward neighborhood organizations rather than individuals and larger organizations, and among and from existing government organizations. However, an underlying idea is that in an effective strategy the result would be a net increase in aggregate power rather than only a redistribution of power. This would come through better prepared

individuals, a stronger metropolitan economy, more successful
neighborhoods in which people can lead successful lives, fewer
resources lost on unsuccessful public programs, and a step toward
learning more productive ways to do things.

Structure

Examination of mission should precede examination of power
arrangements, and both should precede reorganization and resource
decisions. It is not useful to suggest specific organizational changes
for carrying out a metropolitan-scale inner city improvement
strategy. Therefore, this discussion will be brief and more about
ideas and directions than specifics, while observing that the existing
structure not only has not been solved, but has partially caused
inner city problems.

It is here suggested that the fundamental units of organization
in a metropolitan area are the individual, the household, the neighborhood, and the metropolitan area. All other units are useful
inventions whose justification would seem to be based upon some
combination of continued usefulness, effectiveness and represen-
tativeness.

It is clear that metropolitan areas that hope to succeed not only
in inner city improvement, but in environmental, transportation, and
economic development issues need a metropolitan-wide scale and
more sophisticated analysis, policy-making, and implementation
than now exists. Those that don't put some neighborhood and effective metropolitan structure in place will continue to slip on many
fronts. This is not just a matter of the relationship of metropolitan
governance to local government, but also to private and market organization.

In addition, a unit of analysis and planning organization is
needed at the radial geographic sector. Housing markets are
metropolitan, but also, to a significant degree, play out in radial sectors in which market activity, income flows and demographic shifts
are stronger within than among sectors.

Housing markets, low income housing distribution, policy and
funding, job distribution, development patterns and racial segregation and integration should be analyzed and debated by some more
or less formal submetropolitan organizations fitted to these sectors.

The most difficult need is for stronger neighborhoods, in both a
sense-of-community and organizational sense. There needs to be
organization here that not only assumes responsibility from various
levels of government, but from other elements of the private sector
as well. A specific example is the neighborhood owned and
operated real estate company suggested in Chapter Seven.

This report does not propose specific local government reorganization, but suggests some direction. One direction is toward people-oriented, service- and market-based, neighborhood-managed revitalization, and away from a reduction in housing-based revitalization. This also suggests a look at the need for, missions, and organization of community development and housing agencies.

We clearly have more units of local government than are needed, but that may or may not make change worthwhile. A strong system of local service delivery and representation is necessary. However, the inviolability of the existing pattern is probably more evident to those with a vested interest in it, i.e., politicians and bureaucrats, than to the general citizenry. Most citizens would probably favor reorganization and consolidation schemes that retained some community functions and identification while giving up other power in order to achieve more results with fewer resources, politicians and bureaucrats. Someone should do attitudinal research on this.

Myths About Resources

Money may be thought of as a resource. However, it is more usefully thought of as a claim on or power over resources. It mobilizes, along with mission, power and structure, the real resources of labor, muscle and brainpower, ideas, material, machinery, classrooms and facilities. The result of its mobilization may be to create more resources, i.e., a classroom or a factory or research laboratory. Or it may only consume other resources.

The ends and means of this resource mobilization depend upon who has the money. A tax on private money redirects resources toward different ends than when it is left in private hands. Money at different levels of government mobilizes different kinds of resources, i.e., street paving and housing inspection, education, and national defense. Income and wealth distribution and redistribution affect the purpose and kinds of resources that get mobilized.

It would seem that a successful socioeconomic system would be one that directed a high proportion of its resources toward production of more resources, i.e., social, cultural, economic, human and environmental capital. It would also seem that long-lasting, high-quality consumption items would be favored. However, the obsession of learned economists and experienced politicians—with seemingly less important distinctions such as public versus private resource proportions, and with maintaining high rates of consumption—belies that.

Some ideas in this report would require money to implement. More low income housing at perhaps more expensive locations, different approaches to social services, more neighborhood organization, and results-oriented services in low income areas are among them. However, whether more money is needed depends upon how we keep the books.

For example, it is probably the case that within the overall economy, we are already spending more on the consumption of housing than is good for any except the most directly involved housing sectors of the national economy. Needing more resources for low income housing suggests a shift of resources within housing rather than increasing aggregate housing expenditures. Taxing or reducing tax subsidies to high income housing in order to assist low income housing would accomplish this. Assuming that the first bathroom in one house usually has more utility than the fourth in another would also increase aggregate useful output.

While in some methods of economic measurement this might appear as a shift from private to public budgets and therefore not pump up the economy, it would have more or less that same impact on employment and aggregate economic activity, whether spent privately or publicly. To the extent that a tax or excise tax on high income housing is also encouraged, the resulting shift from consumption to productivity investment would be good economic policy. Perhaps it would be more useful than reduced capital gains taxes.

Basing the resource discussion on myths about a shortage economy that can't afford to do public things is one way investment in real economy and community growth is stifled. In fact, we are a very affluent economy that has trouble consuming all the material goods that we can and want to produce. Still, we believe that it is the level of demand for products that limits size and growth. This myth seems to persist in the face of the basic fact of most individual businesses. Given more demand, individual and aggregate economies could produce much more. Thus, seeking new global markets for our products is a current favorite public and private economic development activity.

Saturated or constrained markets for air travel, farm products, hospital beds, personal computers, housing, automobiles, office space, retail space, and middle managers, to name a few, verifies that we are in something other than a shortage economy. Thus, it is not a lack of resources or national impoverishment that keeps us from doing public things. We simply don't want to direct the resources that way.

Another barrier to understanding is the myth that public expenditures diminish economic growth. Some public sector expenditures encourage real economic growth and some do not. Some private sector expenditures stimulate real economic growth and some do not. Not maintaining high standards of education, public safety, health and other public services that represent sound investments in community and economic growth represents the triumph of rhetoric over common sense.

Given appropriate skepticism about systems of central economic planning to direct resources, we should pursue policies and programs that give democracy and capitalism a strong, if imperfect, tendency to use resources in the most productive ways. Some failures of this tendency in both its democratic and capitalistic aspects are construction of huge shopping centers in a saturated retail market; more office space in a saturated office market; continued construction of oversized, underdesigned housing in environmentally sensitive locations while abandoning good existing housing; and homeless people on the streets of the city in the same neighborhoods as abandoned vacant housing. Democratic capitalism still has room for improvement in productive application of resources when it builds excess retail and office space while letting the proportion of its children in poverty increase, and when it fails to maintain global education standards.

Investment in a strong private sector is necessary for global competitiveness, to maintain our standard of living, and to show the world what capitalism can do. Investment in a strong public sector is necessary for global competitiveness, to maintain our quality of living, and to show the world what democratic capitalism can do. In the new global economy, our aggregate national economic strength will increasingly be determined by the strength and global competitiveness of individual regions and metropolitan areas. Achieving this strength is not a matter of balance between public and private investment, but of synergistic investment of resources in the most useful ways. The publicness or privateness of a venture is more a matter of means than ends, i.e., the private sector is reputed to do things more efficiently, so let them do it when that is the case.

Aaron Wildavsky approaches resource allocation somewhat differently (*Speaking Truth to Power*, 370). He brilliantly ties method to purpose, i.e., resources to mission, and reveals why those of different income or political persuasion have difficulty understanding each others' point of view about the meaning of "equity" in the use of resources. Wildavsky discusses three standards of equity used in allocating resources to public goods and services. All can be called "equitable," but the results are vastly different.

The first is market equity in which resources are distributed exactly as derived: the more taxes one pays the more services one receives. The resulting distribution of goods would resemble what the private market would do with no redistribution among income classes or areas or perhaps even individuals if perfectly played out. To each according to his contribution.

The second is equal opportunity equity in which each citizen receives an equal dollar amount of services or even an equal amount of each service, notwithstanding any measure of either contribution or need. This implies some degree of redistribution, and perhaps a community sense that "all children should have the same education opportunity even if upper income families pay a disproportionate share of the cost."

Wildavsky's third standard is equal results—distributing services and resources so that the outcome is equal for each citizen. The idea is that more difficult situations receive more input in order to achieve desired conditions. This implies even more income redistribution and equal opportunity standards if the more difficult conditions are associated with areas or people of lower income. This isn't always the case. For example, more affluent bus riders from distant suburbs usually buy a longer ride than low income riders so a flat, equal results fare favors them, while a zoned-fare system is more nearly a market equity system.

Debate over what to do and how to pay for it tends to be a contest among evidently correct, but contradictory, approaches to equity. "Any fool knows that each citizen should get back in property services what they pay in property taxes" (market equity), just as "any fool knows that we should spend the same amount on each block of street notwithstanding differences in income among neighborhoods" (opportunity equity), or "any fool knows that all the streets should be paved and plowed to the same standard notwithstanding variable engineering difficulties and income differences among neighborhoods" (results equity).

Each of these, market equity, opportunity equity, and results equity can be viewpoints that exclude other viewpoints, though the services standards and income redistribution implications among them are vastly different. Public professionals often accept as the only correct route an industry, trade group, or professional society standard that plays out one or another of Wildavsky's equity standards, without even thinking about the implications.

As in politics, any good conservative knows that emulating the private market and market equity is the way to public sector success, while any good liberal knows that equal opportunity is what democracy is about. Advocates of achievement standards for schools know that equal results are the only way to go. Analysis alone doesn't cut through such clearly "correct," contradictory views, which is why such matters require political compromise rather than only analytical correctness for their resolution.

How might this apply to the resource demands implied by this report? Among ideas included here are metropolitan-wide locations for low income housing, results-oriented service delivery to maintain the human development characteristics of low income areas,

and increased attention to reconnection of low income households
and neighborhoods to metropolitan opportunity in jobs, development, transportation and housing planning.

No one expects that low income shelter will offer the same
luxury and spaciousness as other housing, though the contrary—
that it should not—is an occasionally used red herring in housing
policy debates. Provision of low income housing is not intended to
achieve "results equity" to that degree. I would, however, argue that
while our national legislated housing policy since 1949 has been
"safe, sanitary housing in a decent environment for everyone," our
practices in low income housing have ranged from market equity
for the few that get on the list; to public housing that tries to be safe
and sanitary, but is not usually in a decent environment; to the
1980s belief that not everyone needs shelter.

I would suggest that housing policy and practice should
embrace the results equity standard to the degree that all should
have shelter. Expecting markets alone to achieve that in all cases is
silly. It is further clear that provision for housing safety and sanitation standards for everyone is as necessary in resource allocation as
in regulation.

The public interest in housing results equity then shifts from
the shelter unit to issues of location, neighborhood environment,
and the human development characteristics of low income areas.
While it need not be public policy that low income structures
achieve the same results in space and luxury as private market housing, the standard for the location should be to achieve the same
public safety, public health, education and general neighborhood
conditions, and overall human development results as in higher income areas. Housing should be good enough to be safe, sanitary,
and not be an additional burden. The neighborhood condition expectations should be much higher.

Beyond this, housing policy should emphasize equal opportunity and market equity. Equal opportunity would mean that all
units of local government would be expected to permit and encourage the availability of a full range of housing densities and prices
within their boundaries. This standard is used in a number of states
and is practiced in the Portland metropolitan area under Oregon
legislation and state standards.

A market equity standard would mean little redistribution of
wealth and income among classes, but would suggest no, or relatively low, ceilings on the tax deductibility of housing costs. New
market rate housing would be expected to cover all of its development costs and to pass none of these on to the public sector.

Chapter Six advocates a results approach to public services in
low income and poverty areas in order to keep these areas from
becoming the causes of further poverty. It further suggests that the

most important of these are the basic community services of public safety, public health, education, and maintenance of general public conditions. This requires a results equity standard for services in low income areas and a change of mindset from the present expectation and acceptance of poor results in low income areas. It requires lots of experimentation, flexibility and innovation in how services are delivered. It usually will mean spending more per capita than in other areas and, thus, redistribution of wealth.

A market equity standard for these basic services, particularly education, when we know it perpetuates low income conditions is, in its aggregate effect, discriminatory. An equal opportunity standard, i.e., equal class sizes in all neighborhoods and communities notwithstanding wealth, is less discriminatory and politically practical.

However, to pursue an equal opportunity standard with our current awareness that the outcomes will then be vastly different among neighborhoods, incomes, and racial situations is also discriminatory. Given this knowledge, an equal opportunity standard for education expenditures becomes a conscious decision and de facto social policy that many inner city children will have their life chances curtailed at a very young age.

A results equity standard seems the only one that education, public safety, and health care policy could consider in a forward-looking, affluent, democratic capitalistic society. It must then be examined in fine enough detail to ensure that it begins to come out that way everywhere, including low income neighborhoods.

Resources are the materials used to change the world, or to keep it the same. Control of money gives claim to resources and how they are used. Notwithstanding the temporal vagaries of money flow, an institution that has people who believe in it and themselves and has ideas, materials, natural resources, a healthy natural environment, and effective educational systems that work for everyone, has resources with which to do things. If it is unable to do so because of leadership, political or economic system failures, it is these systems that are weak and failing and need repair or replacement, not the institution or place itself.

Next Steps

Many ideas in this book have been asserted as fact, as what clearly needs to be done. In most cases this accurately represents the author's firm conclusions. However, public policy does not start with conclusions, but with ideas, political philosophy, information, and self-interest. It sometimes proceeds through open discussion to decisions and action.

If a metropolitan-scale strategy for solving inner city problems got on the public agenda as a result of a few people reading this report, that would be a useful outcome. Therefore, one recommendation is that state, metropolitan, and local government form a joint commission to prepare such a strategy and agree upon the assignment of responsibility for carrying out each of its components. The commission should be charged with developing an approach intended to reverse long-term trends of inner city decline; an approach that puts in place a trend of long-term, patient improvement that will have made significant differences by the end of the century; one that gets at fundamental causes and remedies; one that addresses the dynamics of the metropolitan housing market and public policy in creating central city conditions; one as much about people as about the physical condition of places. The commission should have a year to eighteen months to complete their work, enough power to get attention, and enough resources to do a thorough job of examining inner city problems, opportunities, and solutions rather than just another rehash of housing programs.

The new structures, programs and resources being put in place by cities to create partnerships to revitalize neighborhoods will be most successful in strengthening places with early indications of decline, and dealing with the internal market weaknesses of these places. This can address the strategy component of Chapter Seven, improving the market strength of central city neighborhoods.

It is also possible for partnerships to address successfully the human development qualities of low income and poverty neighborhoods. As discussed in Chapter Six, this requires innovative exploration by organizations to deliver "results oriented" services in education, public safety, public health, and general neighborhood condition services that have so much influence on human development in low income neighborhoods.

These strategy elements are appropriately addressed primarily by partnerships of city and neighborhood organizations, with perhaps some resource and enabling legislative assistance from higher levels of government and the private profit and nonprofit sectors. However, in order to get successful results from those city and neighborhood efforts, other elements must be addressed by higher levels of society and government. These should be addressed by state legislation and/or effective metropolitan agencies.

Conclusions

A successful community at any scale—household, neighborhood, town or metropolitan city—is one in which people can lead successful lives. Successful markets, traditions, governance institutions and developments are those which bring about settings for those successful communities and lives to take place. Those that impede individual and community success have failed and should be changed or discarded.

Inner city conditions represent the failure of neighborhoods, markets, institutions and government to provide or even make best efforts to provide a setting in which people who want and attempt to succeed can do so.

It is difficult to change people. It may not be the function of government to change people. However, improving inner city conditions does not require changing people. It requires breaking down the isolation that prevents people from seeing possibilities. It requires removing the barriers that keep them from preparing for and taking advantage of opportunities. It requires secure, healthy, clean neighborhoods in which people's lives are supported rather than threatened and inhibited by their surroundings. It requires education systems that prepare people to succeed either in their community or somewhere else. It requires jobs and access to jobs that are fulfilling enough and pay enough to encourage life. It requires the ability to make choices and some real choice to be made.

Improving inner city conditions does not require deep analysis or fundamental change in human character. If it did, neither government nor any other institution would be able to do it. So we might just as well set about doing what we can do.

We can set about changing the practices, institutions and conditions that increase the incidence of poverty. We can remove public support from and change the market practices and public policies that concentrate and isolate that poverty in the inner city. We can actively increase the residential choices for those who wish to exercise that choice to improve economic, social and educational opportunity.

We can, through traditional community services of public safety, public health, education and maintaining neighborhood conditions, improve the human development characteristics of inner city neighborhoods and keep these places from being a further obstacle to successful living. This requires political and organizational innovation and allocation of resources, a far more appropriate, practical and surmountable challenge than the oft-prescribed remedy of changing human nature.

We can unify metropolitan leadership and form partnerships which believe that these conditions can and should be fundamentally changed rather than tolerated, served and used. It is entirely possible for a forward-looking metropolitan area and city government to develop and put in place a long-term strategy that can alter fundamental causes and bring about lasting improvement in inner city conditions. Such a city would become a model for other cities.

We know a great deal about what works. We need to apply that knowledge at the scale of the problem. Our society and economy have the resources to greatly improve inner city problems and the poverty issues that lie behind them. Failure to do so is a failure of leadership, markets, institutions, and public policy. Changes in these components will set the stage for people to create successful neighborhoods, communities, and metropolitan cities in which people can live successful lives.

Bibliography

Abler, Ronald, John S. Adams, and John R. Borchert. *The Twin Cities of St. Paul and Minneapolis*. Cambridge, MA: Ballinger Publishing Company, 1976.

Adams, John S. *Housing America in the 1980s*. New York: Russell Sage Foundation, 1987.

Borchert, John R. *America's Northern Heartland*. Minneapolis: University of Minnesota Press, 1987.

Bourne, Larry S. *The Geography of Housing*. New York: Halstead Press, 1981.

Brandl, John and Arthur Naftalin. *The Twin Cities Regional Strategy*. St. Paul, MN: Metropolitan Council, 1980.

Byrnes, Carol. Story about New York's paupers' graves on Hart Island. Minneapolis *Star Tribune* 12 December 1990, p. 1.

Cook, Christine, et al. *Expanding Opportunities for Single Parents Through Housing*. Minneapolis, MN: University of Minnesota, 1988.

Downs, Anthony. *The Future of Industrial Cities, An Essay in the New Urban Reality*. Ed. Paul Peterson. Washington, D.C.: The Brookings Institute, 1985.

Downs, Anthony. "The Need for a New Vision of Our Urban Future," excerpted from National Press Club speech, May 31, 1989, reproduced in *City Planning and Management News*. Chicago, IL: American Planning Association, September 1989.

Drucker, Peter F. *The Age of Discontinuity*. New York: Harper & Row, 1968.

Finn, Chester E. Jr. "Ten Tentative Truths," presentation and paper, Center for the American Experiment, Minneapolis, MN, April and June 1990.

Hughes, Mark Allen. *Poverty in Cities*. Washington, D.C.: National League of Cities, 1989.

Kasarda, John D. "Urban Change and Minority Opportunity." *The New Urban Reality*. Ed. Paul Peterson. Washington, D.C.: The Brookings Institute, 1985.

Johnson, Lyndon. July 26, 1967, quoted in "The Report of the National Commission on Civil Disorders," The Kerner

Commission. New York: New York Times Edition, E.P. Dutton and Co., Inc., 1968.

Macdonald, Austin F. *American City Government and Administration*. New York: Thomas Y. Corwell Co., 1929.

Mack, Raymond W. *Segregation in Education, Our Children's Burden*. New York: Random House, 1968.

Martin, Judith A. and David E. Lanegran. *Where We Live, The Residential Districts of Minneapolis and St. Paul*. Minneapolis, MN: University of Minnesota Press, 1983.

McKnight, John L. *The Future of Low Income Neighborhoods and the People Who Reside There*. Evanston, IL: Center for Urban Affairs and Policy Research, Northwestern University, 1989.

Metropolitan Council, *Looking Ahead at Housing*. St. Paul, MN: Metropolitan Council, 1988.

Metropolitan Council, *Changes in the Subsidized Housing Market, 1980-1989*. St. Paul, MN: Metropolitan Council, 1990.

Minneapolis Planning Department. *Comprehensive Law Enforcement Plan*. Minneapolis, MN: Minneapolis Planning Department, 1989.

Minneapolis Planning Department, *Hearing Draft of the Plan for the 1980s*. Minneapolis, MN: Minneapolis Planning Department, 1979.

Murray, Charles. *Losing Ground, American Social Policy 1950-1980*. New York: Basic Books, 1984.

Mumford, Lewis. *The City in History*, San Diego, New York, London: Harcourt Brace Jovanich, 1961.

Orfield, Gary. "Ghettoization and its Alternatives." *The New Urban Reality*. Ed. Paul Peterson. Washington, D.C.: The Brookings Institute, 1985.

Phillips, Kevin. *The Politics of Rich and Poor, Wealth and the American Electorate in the Reagan Aftermath*. New York: Random House, 1990.

Pressman, Steven. "The Feminization of Poverty," *Challenge Magazine*, April 1988: 55-58.

Rosenbaun, James E. and Susan E. Popkin. "The Gautreaux Program: An Experiment in Racial and Economic Integration," The Center Report, Vol. 2, No. 1, Center for Urban Affairs and Policy Research, Northwestern University, Evanston, IL, Spring 1990.

Sawhill, Isabel. "Poverty and the Underclass." *Challenge to Leadership*. Washington, D.C.: The Urban Institute, 1988.

Sternleib, George. Presentation to Minneapolis City Council, Minneapolis, MN, May, 1988.

Terry, Robert. *Leadership, A Preview of the Seventh View*, Hubert H. Humphrey Institute of Public Affairs. Minneapolis, MN: University of Minnesota, 1990.

United States Congress, *Housing Act of 1949*, Pub. L. No. 81-171, c. 338, 63 Stat. 413, Sec. 2 (1949).

Warner, Sam Bass. *Streetcar Suburbs, The Process of Growth, 1870-1900*. Cambridge, MA: Harvard University Press, 1978.

Wildavsky, Aaron. *Speaking Truth to Power, The Art and Craft of Policy Analysis*. New Brunswick, NJ: Transaction Books, 1987.

Wilson, Julius William. "Social Isolation, A New Look at the Problems of Race and Poverty in the Inner City Ghetto," presentation, University of Wisconsin, Madison, WI, 30 May 1990.

Wilson, Julius William. *The Truly Disadvantaged, The Inner City, The Underclass and Public Policy*. Chicago, IL: University of Chicago Press, 1987.